HENRY DEMAREST LLOYD, born in 1847, was the son of a Dutch Reformed Minister. He was raised by an uncle in New York City, and graduated from Columbia University in 1867. After three years as a political reformer, he became an editor of the *Chicago Tribune,* and within three years married the daughter of one of its owners. In 1881 he published "The Story of a Great Monopoly" in the *Atlantic Monthly.* Now moderately famous, he retired from the *Tribune* and devoted his time to writing; he lived on a large income from his own and his wife's capital. His subsequent writings were either defenses of labor or attacks upon privilege and monopoly. IIis first book was *The Strike of Millionaires Against Miners* (1890), and his second was *Wealth Against Commonwealth* (1894). Later articles were eventually published in book form as *Man, the Social Creator* (1906). Lloyd was active in the Populist party and later in Eugene Debs' American Socialist Party. In his last years he spent much time investigating labor conditions in England and the British Dominions.

THOMAS C. COCHRAN, who received his Ph.D. from the University of Pennsylvania, is Professor of the History of the People of the United States at the University of Pennsylvania. Among his many books on American history are RAILROAD LEADERS, 1845-1890; THE AMERICAN BUSINESS SYSTEM; and A BASIC HISTORY OF AMERICAN BUSINESS.

Wealth Against Commonwealth

Henry Demarest Lloyd

Edited and with an Introduction by

THOMAS C. COCHRAN

GREENWOOD PRESS, PUBLISHERS
WESTPORT, CONNECTICUT

Library of Congress Cataloging in Publication Data
Lloyd, Henry Demarest, 1847-1903.
    Wealth against commonwealth.

    Reprint of the ed. published by Prentice-Hall, Engle-
wood Cliffs, N.J., in series: Classics in history series.
    Includes bibliography.
    1. Trusts, Industrial--United States. 2. Standard
Oil Company. I. Title.
[HD2769.O4L8 1976]   338.8'0973   76-000007
ISBN 0-8371-8726-5

Originally published in 1963 by Prentice-Hall, Inc.,
Englewood Cliffs, N.J.

Reprinted with the permission of Prentice-Hall, Inc.

Reprinted in 1976 by Greenwood Press,
a division of Williamhouse-Regency Inc.

Library of Congress Catalog Card Number 76-000007

ISBN 0-8371-8726-5

Printed in the United States of America

Table of Contents

vii

INTRODUCTION

"The Story of a Great Monopoly" appeared in the *Atlantic Monthly* for March, 1881. This severely critical history of the oil trust by Henry Demarest Lloyd, financial editor of the *Chicago Tribune,* made its author a national figure. Each of his succeeding articles was widely read both in England and America. Robert Louis Stevenson, then at the height of his fame, said: "Mr. Lloyd . . . writes the most workmanlike article of any man known to me in America, unless it should be Parkman." [1]

These articles were a prelude to his lengthy book, *Wealth Against Commonwealth.* Published in 1894, this was a detailed and powerful protest against the corruption bred by the unrestrained power of wealth, a warning to the American people against the advance of "business feudalism." With a few minor exceptions the thesis is elaborated by showing the unethical ways in which the trustees of the Standard Oil Company influenced railroads and government.

Although most of the material comes from legislative investigations, hearings, and legal testimony under oath, Lloyd's use of this evidence was attacked by some contemporary reviewers and later historians. The *New York Times* said: "He has neither judicial fairness of mind or self-control. The volume is defaced by passion and is made unwholesome by intolerance." [2] A review in *The Nation,* a mildly conservative publication, condemned Lloyd for exhibiting "such indifference to truth, such incoherence of thought, such intemperance of speech and such violence of passion as to make

[1] Caro Lloyd, *Henry Demarest Lloyd, 1847-1903: A Biography,* 2 vols. (New York: G. P. Putnam's, Sons, 1912), I, 71. Caro Lloyd was Henry's sister.

[2] Allan Nevins, *John D. Rockefeller: The Heroic Age of American Enterprise* (New York: Charles Scribner's Sons, 2 vols., 1940), II, 338.

him an undesirable leader." [3] Professor Nevins attacks Lloyd's use of facts in a particular case as "one of the most dishonest pieces of so-called history I have ever read." [4]

On the other hand, the *Review of Reviews* said Lloyd's "massing of facts was irresistible," and the *Outlook* praised the book as "the most powerful volume on economics since *Progress and Poverty*." [5] Even Professor Nevins admits that while the officers of Standard Oil might have supplied facts to confute many of Lloyd's pages, to do this would have involved making *damaging admissions at many points*, and for this they were not prepared.[6]

Chester McA. Destler, checking 420 of Lloyd's total of 648 references to source material, found only ten inaccuracies in statements, and these in ways "not of great import." Of 241 important undocumented statements, Dr. Destler verified 229 completely, eight partially, and found only four incorrect. Furthermore, "the mistakes modify the narrative to only a slight degree." [7] "But when all allowances are made," judges Destler, "Lloyd's pioneering report on the methods by which the oil monopoly was established and maintained remains substantially unaltered, although later authorities emphasize more the role of economy and efficiency in the rise of Standard Oil." [8]

From all this discussion one is forced to the conclusion that in spite of 535 large pages of text Lloyd's main thesis was obscured both initially and later by arguments over the morals of John D. Rockefeller and the ethics of the Standard Oil Company. Careful examination of Lloyd's pages should lead to a quite different emphasis. He had a much larger context than an attack on one particular corporation. As he explains many times, the control of the economically useful highways of the nation, the railroads, by private corporations put an essential utility in the hands of men motivated by personal profit rather than service to either the public or the stockholders. When corporations shipping over competing roads grew big enough to supply a large part of the through traffic in some commodity, these shippers could play off the railroads against each other in order to gain special rates, could, at times, achieve

[3] *Ibid.*, p. 339.
[4] *Ibid.*, p. 336, n. 11.
[5] *Ibid.*, p. 337.
[6] *Ibid.*, p. 339. Italics added.
[7] Chester McA. Destler, *American Radicalism, 1865-1901*, Connecticut College Press, 1946, p. 144.
[8] *Ibid.*, p. 146.

even more discriminatory results by influencing railroad officers, and could exercise political influence to thwart justice. Standard Oil was selected as an example because its relations with the railroads seemed to cover the whole range of corporate practice dangerous to the public interest, and because there was abundant evidence of the practices in government documents.

Material appearing in government documents is, of course, no more reliable than the men who supplied it. Witnesses testifying under oath may still exaggerate or lie, or be honestly incapable of remembering the correct facts. Judges may give way to emotion in charging juries. Legislative hearings may be guided for political purposes. The sections of *Wealth Against Commonwealth* chosen for this edition are those supported by the evidence that seems most reliable and important. Thus the episode that led to the conviction by a jury of some officials of Vacuum Oil (a subsidiary of Standard) for an attempt to blow up a competing refinery, the account called "most dishonest" by Professor Nevins, has not been reprinted because of the obviously unstable character of the chief witness. To permit pleasant reading, the extracts, totaling about forty percent of the original text, are joined together without indicating omissions. The original chapter numbers have been retained.

Lloyd's minor inaccuracies do not seem important. The case is only incidentally against the trustees and officers of Standard Oil; the chief defendant was American business, called upon to justify its practices and ethics. If the officers of Standard Oil did not bribe a particular legislator or lie in regard to some contract, the business historian of the period knows that other businessmen did. Lloyd's book is a substantially accurate picture of the social dangers in the prevailing business philosophy that a good end justified any means.

These business leaders, if pressed for a justification of their efforts, maintained that they were developing the country and raising the standard of living. Their large profits were ploughed back into further investment in the same or new enterprises. The amount that a few spent on luxurious living was not an important deduction from the gross national product. The basic economic question was: Were they efficient investors of capital?

As essentially a social and moral philosopher Lloyd does not argue this point. Impatient to advance his attack, he often fails to narrate relevant economic history or explain the economic context of events. Like the Count de Boulanger in Anatole France's *Penguin Island*, the independent refiners are always being beaten insensible, only to reappear vigorous and prosperous in the next episode. This illustrates the structural ambiguity in the book that has misled so many reviewers. It is not a satisfactory or coherent study of either railroad rebates or the oil industry, but rather a dramatically presented warning of the menace to public rights and democratic government inherent in a business society of big, monopolistic corporations. The language is often journalistic rather than calmly analytical; the reader sometimes loses the basic argument amid exciting details.

Yet Lloyd deserves a place among America's important social and economic critics. Some earlier, and many later, writers have pointed out that the assumptions of Adam Smith that in a free market private selfishness is public good, or that the "laws" of the market will automatically compel the greatest efficiency, no longer apply when corporations become big enough and few enough to prevent price competition. But none of these writers has so colorfully related the evidence to social issues. Many contemporary writers attacked discriminatory railroad rates, but Lloyd underlined the most extreme examples. Furthermore, he skillfully contrasts his examples with the American cultural traditions of equality of opportunity, protection of individual rights, and verbal honesty.

That Lloyd should be primarily a moralist rather than an economist is explicable from his background. The son of a Dutch Reformed minister who, too independent to keep a post in a church, became a bookseller in Greenwich Village, Lloyd was brought up in a household where serious, morally guided conversation, often focused on a selected subject, was the rule. The impecunious Lloyds lived with Mrs. Lloyd's father, David Demarest, at 27 Washington Place. One of Mrs. Lloyd's brothers who lived next door made the family circle still larger and more engrossing. The Demarests, also strict members of the Dutch Reformed Church, were Republicans by 1860, whereas Henry's paternal grandfather was the Democratic postmaster of nearby Belleville, New Jersey. As a result, the young man, fourteen years old in 1861, heard much of the controversy that ended in the Civil War from very serious protagonists.

While boyhood in New York did not mean full participation in a cosmopolitan culture—the theater and other frivolous amusements were condemned on religious grounds—Henry and his brother and sister were free to read widely and attend other churches. All three became able writers. Good education was also available. One of his professors at Columbia said of Henry Lloyd, "I do not hesitate to say that in liveliness of fancy the author excels all his class fellows and with practice will become a most popular writer." [9] Finishing Columbia College in the class of 1867, he attended the Law School and passed the New York Bar Examinations in 1869.

As a young New York lawyer he was quickly drawn into the struggle against Boss Tweed and Tammany Hall. He became a leader of the Young Men's Association which combined in 1871 with the Committee of Seventy distinguished citizens to help break the power of the Tweed Ring. Secretary of the New York State Committee for Liberal Republicanism in 1872, and a delegate to the national convention of Liberal Republicans, he fought to the end against the disastrous nomination of Horace Greeley. A reporter at the convention characterized the twenty-five-year-old Lloyd as "laboring under the delusion that he was carrying the nation on his young shoulders." [10]

By this time Lloyd had decided that the law was "too technical and traditional." [11] On the other hand, he was "too unconventially and unaffectedly pious to be a minister." [12] Yet he had "a yearning for public distinction," and power.[13] "I want power," he wrote, "I must have power, I could not live if I did not think that I was in some way to be lifted above and upon the insensate masses who flood the stage of life in their passage to oblivion, but I want power unpoisoned by the presence of obligation. Can you think of any avenue to power, more independent . . . more in consonance with such tasks as I describe than Journalism?" [14]

Horace White, one of the famous Midwestern editors, already aware of Lloyd's potential as a journalist, added him to the staff of the *Chicago Tribune*. There Lloyd's career was advanced by the kind of good fortune immortalized in the Horatio Alger stories. Within a year he had married Jennie Bross whose father was one of the owners of the paper. Yet Lloyd's success as Financial Editor of the *Tribune* from 1875 to 1882 and as general editorial writer from 1882 to 1885 was more than warranted by his abilities.

During this period he could have bought a paper of his own and become a publisher as he claimed he wanted to be, but for some

[9] Caro Lloyd, *op. cit.* I, 15.
[10] *Ibid.*, Vol. I, p. 33.
[11] *Ibid.*, p. 39.
[12] *Ibid.*, p. 40.
[13] *Ibid.*, p. 40.
[14] *Ibid.* From a letter to Henry Kennan, a fellow worker in the Liberal Republican Movement.

reason he let opportunities slip by. One may surmise that while Lloyd still liked to think of himself as potentially a man of action, he was by nature a writer and a scholar. Support for such a theory is supplied by his later life. In 1885 he retired from the *Tribune* because of insomnia and nervous troubles and devoted himself chiefly to research and writing at his large home in Winnetka and summer place on Cape Cod.

His support of the anarchists condemned for the Haymarket Square Riot in Chicago in 1886, although nothing but radical utterances could be proved against them, led Lloyd's conservative father-in-law to put his large estate in trust for the Lloyd children, without naming Henry as a trustee. But his wife's income continued to remove worry over money matters. The voluminous research and documentation of *Wealth Against Commonwealth* was facilitated by both secretaries and research assistants.

His comfortable life and success at the *Tribune* are important in evaluating the biases of *Wealth Against Commonwealth*. Lloyd was not an angry young man condemning a system that had denied him success; he was not a poorly paid journalist envying the rich and powerful; he was not a businessman ruined by railroad rebates; he was a successful literary man living in the style of a millionaire, charting the course of social evolution and marshalling the sanctions of American Christian morality from a height above the battle.

In the last two chapters of *Wealth Against Commonwealth* Lloyd moves beyond the railroads and Standard Oil to assess the trends of industrial society and look into the future. These are the chapters for which all the rest of the book had furnished the detailed evidence: The Lloyd position can oversimply be identified with English Fabian Socialism of his day, with the doctrine that "we are to apply the co-operative methods of the post-office and public school to many other common toils, to all toils in which private sovereignty has become through monopoly a despotism over the public . . ." [15] But Lloyd's position is based on moral imperatives rather than on those of economic necessity.

The writing in these chapters is often brilliant and many-faceted. Starting from the premise that "History has taught us nothing if not that men can continue to associate only by laws of association," Lloyd understood the necessity for the advance of governmental controls in American society which has actually taken place during

[15] Henry D. Lloyd, *Wealth Against Commonwealth* (New York: Harper & Row, Publishers, 1894), p. 534.

the succeeding seventy years.[16] Seeing a largely socialized state, democratically controlled as the result, he wrote: "Whether the great change comes with peace or sword, freely through reform or by nature's involuntary forces, is a mere matter of detail, a question of convenience, not the essence of the thing. The change will come." [17]

He saw democracy as an evolving process, first abolishing feudalism, monarchy and slavery, and finally ending monopoly and special privilege in economic life. "Political government by the self-interest of the individual we call anarchy. . . . Politically we are civilized, industrially not yet." [18] "The true law of business is that all must pursue the interests of all." [19]

Unlike the Marxians who preached revolution, his approach was basically that of a liberal reformer. His attitudes clearly anticipated those of the more advanced progressives of the next generation. He called upon the enlightened American citizenry of 1900 to "adopt a policy more dignified and effective than leaving themselves to be kicked along the path of reform by the recoil of their own vices. We must bring the size of our morality," he warned, "up to the size of our cities, corporations and combinations, or these will be brought down to fit our half-grown virtue." [20]

If the people failed to meet the challenge of the times, however, America could go the way of earlier civilizations. "If our civilization is destroyed, as Macaulay predicted, it will not be by his barbarians from below. Our barbarians come from above . . . Without restraints of culture, experience, the pride or even the inherited caution of class or rank, these men, intoxicated, think they are the wave instead of the float." [21] Lloyd did not underestimate the problem. Aware of the ambiguities and contradictions in national culture, he believed that one set of American ideals were "incarnating themselves in men born to command. What these men are we have made them. . . . The conclusion is irresistible that men so given the lead are the representatives of the real 'spirit of the age,' and that the protestants against them are not representatives of our time—are at the best but intimators of times which may be." [22]

Wealth Against Commonwealth did not seem to create a powerful

---

[16] *Ibid.*, p. 522.
[17] *Ibid.*, p. 521.
[18] *Ibid.*, p. 496.
[19] *Ibid.*, pp. 495-496.
[20] *Ibid.*, p. 518.
[21] *Ibid.*, p. 510.
[22] *Ibid.*, pp. 513, 514.

immediate reaction. Washington Gladden, pioneer preacher of the
Social Gospel, was surprised "that Lloyd's book has not caused more
excitement. I hope and trust it is doing its work silently; but it
surprises me that it does not cause an insurrection. We must wait.
The day of judgment will come." [23] Perhaps in the excitement of
labor disputes, free silver, and agrarian protest in the two years
following publication, Lloyd's message seemed slightly remote. But
the Progressive Movement from 1900 on began translating Lloyd's
admonitions into what he had referred to as "epigrams of practice." [24] Within twenty years, enforcement of antitrust laws, strict
regulation of railroads, conservation of natural resources, and social
legislation started to move society along the road Lloyd had hoped
it would travel.

Dying in September 1903, Lloyd took no significant part in Progressive politics. In any case, his influence would have been from
the left, outside the ranks of either the Republican or Democratic
party. In 1896 and 1900 he voted Socialist, but his disbelief in the
inevitability of class struggle prevented him from becoming a party
member. One of his last manuscripts was an explanation of why he
had finally decided that supporting the Socialist Party was the best
expedient. He never finished the final draft.

[23] Caro Lloyd, *op. cit.*, I, 200.
[24] Henry Lloyd, *Wealth*, p. 522.

I

"There Are None"—"They Are Legion"

The world, enriched by thousands of generations of toilers and thinkers, has reached a fertility which can give every human being a plenty undreamed of even in the Utopias. But between this plenty ripening on the boughs of our civilization and the people hungering for it step the "cornerers," the syndicates, trusts, combinations, with the cry of "over-production"—too much of everything. Holding back the riches of earth, sea, and sky from their fellows who famish and freeze in the dark, they declare to them that there is too much light and warmth and food. They assert the right, for their private profit, to regulate the consumption by the people of the necessaries of life, and to control production, not by the needs of humanity, but by the desires of a few for dividends. The coal syndicate thinks there is too much coal. There is too much iron, too much lumber, too much flour—for this or that syndicate.

The majority have never been able to buy enough of anything; but this minority have too much of everything to sell.

Liberty produces wealth, and wealth destroys liberty. "The splendid empire of Charles V.," says Motley, "was erected upon the grave of liberty." Our bignesses, cities, factories, monopolies, fortunes, which are our empires, are the obesities of an age gluttonous beyond its powers of digestion. Mankind are crowding upon each other in the centres, and struggling to keep each other out of the feast set by the new sciences and the new fellowships. Our size has got beyond both our science and our conscience. The vision of the railroad stockholder is not far-sighted enough to see into the office of the General Manager; the people cannot reach across even a ward of a city to rule their rulers; Captains of Industry "do not

9

know" whether the men in the ranks are dying from lack of food
and shelter; we cannot clean our cities nor our politics; the locomotive has more man-power than all the ballot-boxes, and mill-
wheels wear out the hearts of workers unable to keep up beating to
their whirl. If mankind had gone on pursuing the ideals of the
fighter, the time would necessarily have come when there would
have been only a few, then only one, and then none left. This is
what we are witnessing in the world of livelihoods. Our ideals of
livelihood are ideals of mutual deglutition. We are rapidly reaching
the stage where in each province only a few are left; that is the key
to our times. Beyond the deep is another deep. This era is but a
passing phase in the evolution of industrial Caesars, and these
Caesars will be of a new type—corporate Caesars.

For those who like the perpetual motion of a debate in which
neither of the disputants is looking at the same side of the shield,
there are infinite satisfactions in the current controversy as to
whether there is any such thing as "monopoly." "There are none,"
says one side. "They are legion," says the other. "The idea that
there can be such a thing is absurd," says one, who with half a
dozen associates controls the source, the price, the quality, the
quantity of nine-tenths of a great necessary of life. But "There will
soon be a trust for every production, and a master to fix the price
for every necessity of life," said the Senator who framed the United
States Anti-Trust Law. This difference as to facts is due to a difference in the definitions through which the facts are regarded. Those
who say "there are none" hold with the Attorney-General of the
United States and the decision he quotes from the highest Federal
court which has yet passed on this question[1] that no one has a
monopoly unless there is a "disability" or "restriction" imposed by
law on all who would compete. A syndicate that had succeeded in
bottling for sale all the air of the earth would not have a monopoly
in this view, unless there were on the statute-books a law forbidding
every one else from selling air. No others could get air to sell; the
people could not get air to breathe, but there would be no monopoly because there is no "legal restriction" on breathing or selling
the atmosphere.

Excepting in the manufacture of postage-stamps, gold dollars, and
a few other such cases of a "legal restriction," there are no monopolies according to this definition. It excludes the whole body of
facts which the people include in their definition, and dismisses a

[1] Annual Report Attorney-General of the United States, 1893.

great public question by a mere play on words. The other side of
the shield was described by Judge Barrett, of the Supreme Court of
New York. A monopoly he declared to be "any combination the
tendency of which is to prevent competition in its broad and general
sense, and to control and thus at will enhance prices to the detriment of the public. . . . Nor need it be permanent or complete. It
is enough that it may be even temporarily and partially successful.
The question in the end is, Does it inevitably tend to public
injury?" [2]

Those who insist that "there are none" are the fortunate ones
who came up to the shield on its golden side. But common usage
agrees with the language of Judge Barrett, because it exactly fits a
fact which presses on common people heavily, and will grow heavier
before it grows lighter.

The committee of Congress investigating trusts in 1889 did not
report any list of these combinations to control markets, "for the
reason that new ones are constantly forming, and that old ones are
constantly extending their relations so as to cover new branches of
the business and invade new territories."

It is true that such a list, like a dictionary, would begin to be
wrong the moment it began to appear. But though only an instan-
taneous photograph of the whirlwind, it would give an idea, to be
gained in no other way, of a movement shadowing two hemispheres.
In an incredible number of the necessaries and luxuries of life, from
meat to tombstones, some inner circle of the "fittest" has sought,
and very often obtained, the sweet power which Judge Barrett
found the sugar trust had: It "can close every refinery at will, close
some and open others, limit the purchases of raw material (thus
jeopardizing, and in a considerable degree controlling, its production), artificially limit the production of refined sugar, enhance the
price to enrich themselves and their associates at the public expense, and depress the price when necessary to crush out and
impoverish a foolhardy rival."

Many thousands of millions of dollars are represented in these
centralizations. It is a vast sum, and yet is but a minority of our
wealth.

Laws against these combinations have been passed by Congress
and by many of the States. There have been prosecutions under

[2] People of the State of New York vs. The North River Sugar Refining Company. Supreme Court of New York—at Circuit (January 9, 1889). Trusts, New
York Senate, 1889, p. 278.

them by the State and Federal governments. The laws and the law-suits have alike been futile.

In a few cases names and form of organization have been changed, in consequence of legal pursuit. The whiskey, sugar, and oil trusts had to hang out new signs. But the thing itself, the will and the power to control markets, livelihoods, and liberties, and the tolera-tion of this by the public—this remains unimpaired; in truth, facilitated by the greater secrecy and compactness which have been the only results of the appeal to law.

The Attorney-General of the national government gives a large part of his annual report for 1893 to showing "what small basis there is for the popular impression" "that the aim and effect of this statute" (the Anti-Trust Law) "are to prohibit and prevent those aggregations of capital which are so common at the present day, and which sometimes are on so large a scale as to practically control all the branches of an extensive industry." This executive says of the action of the "co-ordinate" Legislature: "It would not be useful, even if it were possible, to ascertain the precise purposes of the framers of the statute." He is the officer charged with the duty of directing the prosecutions to enforce the law; but he declares that since, among other reasons, "all ownership of property is a mo-nopoly, . . . any literal application of the provisions of the statute is out of the question." Nothing has been accomplished by all these appeals to the legislatures and the courts, except to prove that the evil lies deeper than any public sentiment or public intelligence yet existent, and is stronger than any public power yet at call.

What we call Monopoly is Business at the end of its journey. The concentration of wealth, the wiping out of the middle classes, are other names for it. To get it is, in the world of affairs, the chief end of man.

There are no solitary truths, Goethe says, and monopoly—as the greatest business fact of our civilization, which gives to business what other ages gave to war and religion—is our greatest social, political, and moral fact.

The men and women who do the work of the world have the right to the floor. Everywhere they are rising to "a point of informa-tion." They want to know how our labor and the gifts of nature are being ordered by those whom our ideals and consent have made Captains of Industry over us; how it is that we, who profess the religion of the Golden Rule and the political economy of service for service, come to divide our produce into incalculable power and pleasure for a few, and partial existence for the many who are the fountains of these powers and pleasures. This book is an attempt to help the people answer these questions. It has been quarried out of official records, and it is a venture in realism in the world of realities. Decisions of courts and of special tribunals like the Interstate Commerce Commission, verdicts of juries in civil and criminal cases, reports of committees of the State Legislatures and of Congress, oath-sworn testimony given in legal proceedings and in official inquiries, corrected by rebutting testimony and by cross-examination —such are the sources of information.

Full and exact references are given throughout for the guidance of the investigator. The language of witnesses, judges, and official reports has been repeated verbatim, except for the avoidance of the surplusage and reduplication usual in such literature, and that, to permit the use of the dialogue form, the construction has been changed from the third person to the first in quotations from evidence. With these qualifications, wherever quotation marks have been used, the transcription is word for word. Evidence from such sources is more exact, circumstantial, and accurate than that upon which the mass of historical literature is founded.

To give the full and official history of numbers of these combinations, which are nearly identical in inspiration, method, and result, would be repetition. Only one of them, therefore, has been treated in full—the oil trust. It is the most successful of all the attempts to put gifts of nature, entire industries, and world markets under one hat. Its originators claim this precedence. It was, one of its spokesmen says, "the parent of the trust system." [3] It is the best illustration of a movement which is itself but an illustration of the spirit of the age.

[3] *Combinations,* by S. C. T. Dodd, p. 19.

V

Striking Oil

It was an American idea to "strike oil." Those who knew it as the "slime" of Genesis, or used it to stick together the bricks of the Tower of Babel, or knelt to it in the fire temples, were content to take it as it rose, the easy gift of nature, oozing forth on brook or spring. But the American struck it.

The world, going into partial eclipse on account of the failing supply of whale oil, had its lamps all ready for the new light, and industries beyond number needed only an expansion of the supply.

The American manufacturers were making kerosene as early as 1856 from Scotch coal,[1] imported at a cost of $20 to $25 a ton, and getting experts like Silliman to analyze petroleum, in the hope that somehow a supply of it might be got. By 1860 there were sixty-four of these manufactories in the United States. "A crowd of obscure inventors," says Felix Foucon, in the *Revue des Deux Mondes,* "with unremitting labors perfected the lamp—when it was premature to dream that illumination by mineral oil should become universal." All was ready, as the eminent English geologist, Binney, said, "for the start of the vast American petroleum trade." It was not a lack of knowledge, but a lack of petroleum, that hampered the American manufacturer before 1860.[2] The market, the capital, the consumer, the skilled labor, the inventions, and science were all waiting for "Colonel" Drake.

With Drake's success in "striking oil" came to an end the period, lasting thousands of years, of fire temples, sweep and bucket, Seneca oil; and came to an end, also, the Arcadian simplicity of the old

[1] "Petroleum and Its Products," by S. F. Peckham, U.S. Census, 1885, p. 159.
[2] *Ibid.,* p. 160.

14

times—old though so recent—in which Professor Silliman[3] could say, "It is not monopolized by any one, but is carried away freely by all who care to collect it."

The oil age begins characteristically. As soon as Drake's well had made known its precious contents, horses began running, and telegrams flying, and money passing to get possession of the oil lands for the few who knew from those who did not know. The primitive days when "it was not monopolized by any one" were over. Thousands of derricks rose all over the territory, and oil scouts pushed with their compasses through the forests of the wilderness in all directions. Wells were bored all over Europe, as well as America, wherever traces of oil showed themselves, sometimes so close together that when one was pumped it would suck air from the other.

As soon as the petroleum began to flow out of the ground, refineries started up at every available place. They were built near the wells, as at Titusville and Oil City, and near the centres of transportation, such as Pittsburg and Buffalo, and near the points of export, as Philadelphia, Baltimore, New York. Numbers of little establishments appeared on the Jersey flats opposite New York.

There was plenty of oil for every one; at one time in 1862 it was only ten cents a barrel. The means of refining it had long before been found by science and were open to all; and even poor men building little stills could year by year add on to their works, increase their capital, and acquire the self-confidence and independence of successful men. The business was one of the most attractive possible to capital. "There is no handsomer business than this is," said one of the great merchants of New York. "You can buy the (crude) oil one week, and sell it the next week refined, and you can imagine the quantity of business that can be done." Men who understood the business, he said, "if they had not the capital could get all of the money they wanted." [4]

Before the panic of 1873—days of buoyant general prosperity, with no commercial revulsion for a cause—the citizens of this industry began to suffer a wholesale loss of property and business among the refineries in New York, Pittsburg, Cleveland, and elsewhere, the wells of the oil valleys, and the markets at home and abroad.

To the building of refineries succeeded the spectacle—a strange

[3] Silliman: Benjamin Silliman (1779-1864) was an outstanding American chemist and famous professor at Yale in the first half of the nineteenth century. [T.C.]
[4] Testimony of Simon Bernheimer, New York Assembly "Hepburn" Report, 1879, p. 3549 and following.

one for so new a business—of the abandonment and dismantling of refineries by the score. The market for oil, crude and refined, which had been a natural one, began to move erratically, by incalculable influences. It went down when it should have gone up according to all the known facts of the situation, and went up when it should have gone down. This sort of experience, defying ordinary calculations and virtues, made business men gamblers.

"We began speculating in the hope that there would be a change some time or other for the better," testified one who had gone into the business among the first, and with ample capital and expert skill.[5]

Where every one else failed, out of this havoc and social disorder one little group of half a dozen men were rising to the power and wealth which have become the marvel of the world. The first of them came tardily into the field about 1862. He started a little refinery in Cleveland, hundreds of miles from the oil wells. The sixty and more manufacturers who had been able to plant themselves before 1860, when they had to distil coal into petroleum before they could refine petroleum into kerosene, had been multiplied into hundreds by the arrival of petroleum ready made from below. Some of the richest and most successful business men of the country had preceded him and were flourishing.[6] He had been a bookkeeper, and then a partner, in a very small country-produce store in Cleveland. As described by his counsel some years later, he was a "man of brains and energy without money." With him were his brother and an English mechanic. The mechanic was bought out later, as all the expert skill needed could be got for wages, which were cheaper than dividends.[7] Two or three years later another partner was added, who began life as "a clerk in a country store,"[8] and had been in salt and lumber in the West. A young man, who had been in the oil region only eleven years, and for two of the eleven had been errand-boy and bookkeeper in a mixed oil and merchandise business,[9] a lawyer, a railroad man, a cotton broker, a farm laborer who had become refiner, were admitted at various times into the ruling coterie.

[5] Testimony, Trusts, Congress, 1888, p. 214.
[6] Testimony of Simon Bernheimer, New York Assembly "Hepburn" Report, 1879, p. 3548.
[7] Testimony, Freight Discriminations, Ohio House of Representatives, 1879, pp. 184-5.
[8] Testimony, Trusts, Congress, 1888, p. 304.
[9] Testimony, Pennsylvania Tax Case, 1883, p. 486.

The revolution which revolved all the freemen of this industry down a vortex had no sooner begun than the public began to show its agitation through every organ. The spectacle of a few men at the centre of things, in offices rich with plate glass and velvet plush, singing a siren song which drew all their competitors to bankruptcy or insanity or other forms of "co-operation," did not progress, as it might have done a hundred years ago, unnoticed save by those who were the immediate sufferers. The new democracy began questioning the new wealth. Town meetings, organizations of trades and special interests, grand juries, committees of State legislatures and of the United States Senate and House of Representatives, the civil and criminal courts, have been in almost constant action and inquiry since and because.

It was before the Committee of Commerce of the National House of Representatives in 1872 that the first authentic evidence was obtained of the cause of the singular ruin which was overwhelming so fair a field. This investigation in 1872 was suppressed after it had gone a little way. Congress said, Investigate. Another power said, Don't investigate. But it was not stopped until the people had found out that they and the production, refining, and transportation of their oil—the whole oil industry, not alone of the valleys where the petroleum was found, but of the districts where it was manufactured, and the markets where it was bought and sold, and the ports from which it was shipped abroad—had been made the subject of a secret "contract" [10] between certain citizens. The high contracting parties to this treaty for the disposal of an industrial province were, on one side, all the great railroad companies, without whose services the oil, crude or refined, could not be moved to refineries, markets, or ports of shipment on river, lake, or ocean. On the other side was a body of thirteen men, "not one of whom lived in the oil regions, or was an owner of oil wells or oil lands," who had associated themselves for the control of the oil business under the winning name of the South Improvement Company. [11]

By this contract the railroads had agreed with this company of citizens as follows:

1. To double freight rates.
2. Not to charge them the increase.

[10] This contract is printed in full in Exhibits, New York Assembly "Hepburn" Report, 1879, pp. 418-51, and Trust Report, Congress, 1888, pp. 357-61.
[11] Trusts, Congress, 1888, p. 353.

3. To give them the increase collected from all competitors.
4. To make any other changes of rates necessary to guarantee their success in business.
5. To destroy their competitors by high freight rates.
6. To spy out the details of their competitors' business.

The increase in rates in some cases was to be more than double.[12] These higher rates were to be ostensibly charged to all shippers, including the thirteen members of the South Improvement Company; but that fraternity only did not have to pay them really. All, or nearly all, the increase it paid was to be paid back again—a "rebate." [13] The increase paid by every one else—"on all transported by other parties"—was not paid back. It was to be kept, but not by the railroads. These were to hand that, too, over to the South Improvement Company.

This secret arrangement made the actual rate of the South Improvement Company much lower—sometimes half, sometimes less than half, what all others paid. The railroad officials were not to collect these enhanced freight rates from the unsuspecting subjects of this "contract" to turn them into the treasury of the railroads. They were to give them over to the gentlemen who called themselves "South Improvement Company." The "principle" was that the railroad was not to get the benefit of the additional charge it made to the people. No matter how high the railroads put the rates to the community, not the railroads, but the Improvement Company, was to get the gain. The railroads bound themselves to charge every one else the highest nominal rates mentioned. "They shall not be less," was the stipulation. They might be more up to any point; but less they must not be.[14]

To pay money to the railroads for them to pay back was seen to be a waste of time, and it was agreed that the South Improvement Company for its members should deduct from the ostensible rate the amount to be refunded, and pay the railroads only the difference. Simplification could not go further. The South Improvement Company was not even to be put to the inconvenience of waiting for the railroads to collect and render to it the tribute exacted for its benefit from all the other shippers. It was given the right to figure out for its members what the tribute would amount to, and pay it to them out of the money they owed the railroads for freight,

[12] Art. 2, sec. 3.   [13] Art. 2, sec. 4.
[14] Art. 2, sec. 5.

and then pay the railroad what was left, if there was any left.[15] The railroads agreed to supply them with all the information needed for thus figuring out the amount of this tribute, and to spy out for them besides other important details of their competitors' business. They agreed to make reports every day to the South Improvement Company of all the shipments by other persons, with full particulars as to how much was shipped, who shipped, and to whom, and so on.[16]

The detective agency thus established by the railroads to spy out the business of a whole trade was to send its reports "daily to the principal office" of the thirteen gentlemen. If the railroads, forgetting their obligations to the thirteen disciples, made any reduction in any manner to anybody else, the company, as soon as it was found out, could deduct the same amount from its secret rate.[17] If the open rate to the public went down, the secret rate was to go down as much. For the look of things, it was stipulated that any one else who could furnish an equal amount of transportation should have the same rates;[18] but the possibility that any one should ever be able to furnish an equal amount of transportation was fully taken care of in another section clinching it all.

The railway managers, made kings of the road by the grant to them of the sovereign powers of the State, convenanted, in order to make their friends kings of light, that they would "maintain the business" of the South Improvement Company "against loss or injury by competition," so that it should be "a remunerative" and "a full and regular business," and pledged themselves to put the rates of freight up or down, as might be "necessary to overcome such competition." [19] Contracts to this effect, giving the South Improvement Company the sole right for five years to do business between the oil wells and the rest of the world, were made with it by the Erie, the New York Central, the Lake Shore and Michigan Southern, the Pennsylvania, the Atlantic and Great Western, and their connections, thus controlling the industry north, south, east, west, and abroad. The contracts in every case bound all the roads owned or leased by the railroads concerned.[20] The contracts were duly signed, sealed, and delivered. On the oil business of that year, as one of the members of the committee of Congress figured out from the testimony, the railroad managers could collect an increase of $7,500,-

[15] Art. 2, Sec. 4.   [16] Art. 2, Sec. 8.
[17] Art. 2, Sec. 5.   [18] Art. 3.
[19] Art. 4.
[20] Exhibits, New York Assembly "Hepburn" Report, pp. 418-51.

ooo in freights, of which they were to hand over to the South Improvement Company $6,000,000, and pay into the treasury of their employers—the railways—only $1,500,000.

The contract was signed for the New York Central and Hudson River Railroad by its vice-president, but this agreement to kill off a whole trade was too little or too usual to make any impression on his mind. When publicly interrogated about it he could not remember having seen or signed it.[21]

"The effect of this contract," the vice-president of the Erie Railway Company was asked, "would have been a complete monopoly in the oil-carrying trade?"

"Yes, sir; a complete monopoly." [22]

Of the thirteen members of the South Improvement Company which was to be given this "complete monopoly," ten were found later to be active members of the oil trust. They were then seeking that control of the light of the world which it has obtained. Among these ten were the president, vice-president, treasurer, secretary, and a majority of the directors of the oil trust into which the improvement company afterwards passed by transmigration. Any closer connection there could not be. One was the other.

The ablest and most painstaking investigation which has ever been had in this country into the management of the railroads found and officially reported to the same effect:

"The controlling spirits of both organizations being the same." [23]

The freight rates were raised as agreed and without notice. Rumors had been heard of what was coming. The public would not believe anything so incredible. But the oil regions were electrified by the news, February 26, that telegrams had been sent from railroad headquarters to their freight agents advising them of new rates, to take effect immediately, making the cost of shipping oil as much again as it had been. The popular excitement which broke out on the same day and "raged like a violent fever" became a national sensation. The Titusville *Morning Herald* of March 20, 1872, announces that "the railroads to the oil regions have already put up their New York freight from $1.25 to $2.84, an advance of over one hundred per cent." Asked what reason the railroads gave for increasing their rates, a shipper said, "They gave no reason; they

²¹ New York Assembly "Hepburn" Report, 1879, p. 1566.
²² Testimony, Erie Investigation, New York Assembly, 1873, p. 300.
²³ New York Assembly "Hepburn" Report, 1879, p. 42.

telegraphed the local roads to put up the rates immediately." This advance, the superintendents of the railroads told complaining shippers, had been made under the direction of the South Improvement Company, and they had been instructed to make their monthly collections of oil freights from that concern.

The evidence even seems to show that the South Improvement Company was so anxious for the dance of death to begin that it got the freight agents by personal influence to order the increased rates before the time agreed upon with the higher officials. Strenuous efforts were made to have the public believe that the contracts, though sealed, signed, delivered, and put into effect, as the advance in rates most practically demonstrated, had really not been put into effect. The quibbles with which the president of the South Improvement Company sought to give that impossible color to the affair before the committee of Congress drew upon him more than one stinging rebuke from the chairman of the committee.

"During your whole examination there has not been a direct answer given to a question." "I wish to say to you," said the chairman, "that such equivocation is unworthy of you."

The plea needs no answer, but if it did, the language of the railroad men themselves supplies one that cannot be bettered. To the representatives of the people, who had telegraphed them for information "at once, as the excitement is intense, and we fear violence and destruction of property," General McClellan, of the Atlantic and Great Western, replied that the contract was "cancelled"; President Clark, of the Lake Shore, that it was "formally abrogated and cancelled"; Chairman Homer Ramsdell, of the Erie, that it was "abrogated"; Vice-president Thomas Scott, of the Pennsylvania Railroad, that it was "terminated officially";[24] Vice-president Vanderbilt, of the New York Central and Hudson River Railroad, that it was "cancelled with all the railroads."

Contracts that were not complete and in force would not need to be "cancelled" and "abrogated" and "terminated." These announcements were backed up by a telegram from the future head of the oil trust then incubating, in which he said of his company: "This company holds no contracts with the railroad companies."[25] But in 1879 its secretary, called upon by the Ohio Legislature to produce

[24] New York Assembly "Hepburn" Report, 1879, Exhibits, p. 418.
[25] Report of the Executive Committee of the Petroleum Producers' Union, 1872, p. 23.

the contracts the company had with the railroads, showed, among others, one covering the very date of this denial in 1872.[26]

Before Congress the South Improvement Company sought to shelter themselves behind the plea that "their calculation was to get all the refineries in the country into the company. There was no difference made, as far as we were concerned, in favor of or against any refinery; they were all to come in alike."

How they "were all to be taken in" the contract itself showed. It bound the South Improvement Company "to expend large sums of money in the purchase of works for refining," and one of the reasons given by the railroads for making the contract was "to encourage the outlay." Upon what footing buyer and seller would meet in these purchases when the buyer had a secret arrangement like this with the owners of the sole way to and from wells, refineries, and markets, one does not need to be "a business man" to see. The would-be owners had a power to pry the property of the real owners out of their hands.

One of the Cleveland manufacturers who had sold was asked why he did so by the New York Legislature. They had been very prosperous, he said; their profits had been $30,000 to $45,000 a year; but their prosperity had come to a sudden stop.[27]

"From the time that it was well understood in the trade that the South Improvement Company had . . . grappled the entire transportation of oil from the West to the seaboard . . . we were all kind of paralyzed, perfectly paralyzed; we could not operate. . . . The South Improvement Company, or some one representing them, had a drawback of a dollar, sometimes seventy cents, sometimes more, sometimes less, and we were working against that difference." [28]

It was a difference, he said, which destroyed their business.

He went to the officials of the Erie and of the New York Central to try to get freight rates that would permit him to continue in business. "I got no satisfaction at all," he said; "I am too good a friend of yours," said the representative of the New York Central, "to advise you to have anything further to do with this oil trade."

"Do you pretend that you won't carry for me at as cheap a rate as you will carry for anybody else?"

"I am but human," the freight agent replied.

[26] Testimony, Ohio House of Representatives, 1879, p. 257.
[27] Testimony, New York Assembly "Hepburn" Report, 1879, p. 2525.
[28] Testimony, New York Assembly "Hepburn" Report, 1879, p. 2527.

He saw the man who was then busily organizing the South Improvement Company. He was non-committal. "I got no satisfaction, except 'You better sell, you better get clear.' Kind of *sub rosa:* 'Better sell out, no help for it.' "

His firm was outside the charmed circle, and had to choose between selling and dying. Last of all, he had an interview with the president of the all-conquering oil company, in relation to the purchase of their works. "He was the only party that would buy. He offered me fifty cents on the dollar, on the construction account, and we sold out. . . . He made this expression, I remember: 'I have ways of making money that you know nothing of.' "

For the works, which were producing $30,000 to $45,000 a year profit, and which they considered worth $150,000, they received $65,000.

"Did you ascertain in the trade," he was asked, "what was the average rate that was paid for refineries?"

"That was about the figure. . . . Fifty cents on the dollar."

"It was that or nothing, was it not?"

"That or nothing."

The freight rates had been raised in February. This sale followed in three weeks.

"I would not have sold out," he told the Legislature, "if I could have got a fair show with the railways. My business, instead of being an enterprise to buy and sell, became degraded into running after the railways and getting an equal chance with others." [29]

"The only party that would buy" gave his explanation a few years later of the centralization of this business.

"Some time in the year 1872," he swore, "when the refining business of the city of Cleveland was in the hands of a number of small refiners, and was unproductive of profit, it was deemed advisable by many of the persons engaged therein, for the sake of economy, to concentrate the business, and associate their joint capital therein. The state of the business was such at that time that it could not be retained profitably at the city of Cleveland, by reason of the fact that points nearer the oil regions were enjoying privileges not shared by refiners at Cleveland, and could produce refined oil at a much less rate than could be done at this point. It was a well-understood fact at that time among refiners that some arrangement would have to be made to economize and concentrate the business, or ruinous losses would not only occur to the refiners

[29] Testimony, New York Assembly "Hepburn" Report, 1879, pp. 2525-35.

themselves, but ultimately Cleveland, as a point of refining oil, would have to be abandoned. At that time those most prominently engaged in the business here consulted together, and as a result thereof several of the refiners conveyed" to his company, then as always the centre of the centralization, "their refineries, and had the option, in pay therefor, to take stock" in this company, "at par, or to take cash." This company, he continued, "had no agency in creating this state of things which made that change in the refining business necessary at that time, but the same was the natural result of the trade, nor did it in the negotiations which followed use any undue or unfair means, but in all cases, to the general satisfaction of those whose refineries were acquired, the full value thereof, either in stock or cash, was paid as the parties preferred." [30]

The producers were not to fare any better than the refiners. The president of the South Improvement Company said to a representative of the oil regions substantially: "We want you producers to make out a correct statement of the average production of each well, and the exact cost per barrel to produce the oil. Then we propose to allow you a fair price for the oil."

Within forty-eight hours after the freight rates were raised, according to the programme, "the entire business of the oil regions," the Titusville *Herald,* March 20, 1872, reported, "became paralyzed. Oil went down to a point seventy cents below the cost of production. The boring of new wells is suspended, existing wells were shut down. The business in Cleveland stopped almost altogether. Thousands of men were thrown out of work."

The people rose. Their uprising and its justification were described to the Pennsylvania Constitutional Convention of 1873 by a brilliant "anti-monopolist," "a rising lawyer" of Franklin, Venango Co. The principal subject to which he called the attention of his fellow-members was the South Improvement Company, and the light it threw on the problems of livelihood and liberty. Quoting the decision of the Pennsylvania Supreme Court in the Sanford case,[31] he said:

That is the law in Pennsylvania to-day. But in spite of this decision, and in spite of the law, we well know that almost every railroad in this State has been in the habit, and is to-day in the habit, of granting special privileges to individuals, to companies in which the directors

[30] Standard Oil Company *vs.* W. C. Scofield *et al.* Court of Common Pleas, Cuyahoga County, Ohio. Affidavit of the President of the Standard Oil Company.
[31] 11 Harris.

of such railroads are interested, to particular business, and to particular localities. We well know that it is their habit to break down
certain localities, and build up others, to break down certain men in
business and to build up others, to monopolize certain business themselves by means of the numerous corporations which they own and
control, and all this in spite of the law, in defiance of the law.

The South Improvement Company's scheme would give that corporation the monopoly of the entire oil business of this State, amount-
ing to $20,000,000 a year. That corporation was created by the Penn-
sylvania Legislature along with at least twenty others, under the name
of improvement companies, within a few years past, all of which corporations contain the names as original corporators of men who may
be found in and about the office of the Pennsylvania Railroad Company, in Philadelphia, when not lobbying at Harrisburg. The railroads
took but one of those charters which they got from the Legislature,
and by means of that struck a deadly blow at one of the greatest interests of the State. Their scheme was contrary to law, but before the
legal remedy could have been applied, the oil business would have
lain prostrate at their feet, had it not been prevented by an uprising
of the people, by the threatenings of a mob, if you please, by threaten-
ing to destroy property, and by actually commencing to destroy the
property of the railroad company, and had the companies not cancelled the contract which Scott and Vanderbilt and others had entered into, I venture to say there would not have been one mile of
railroad track left in the County of Venango—the people had come
to that pitch of desperation. . . . Unless we can give the people a
remedy for this evil of discriminations in freight, they will sooner or
later take the remedy into their own hands.[32]

Soon after this attorney for the people was promoted from the
poor pay of patriotism to a salary equal to that of the President of
the United States, and to the place of counsel for the principal
members of the combination, whose inwardness he had descried
with such hawk-eye powers of vision. Later, as their counsel, he
drafted the famous trust agreement of 1882.

The South Improvement Company was formed January 2d. The
agreement with the railroads was evidently already worked out in
its principal details, for the complicated contracts were formally
signed, sealed, and delivered January 18th. The agreed increase of
freights went into effect February 26th. The pacific insurrection of
the people began with an impromptu mass-meeting at Titusville
the next day, February 27th. Influential delegations, or committees,
on transportation, legislation, conference with press, pipe lines,
arresting of drilling, etc., were set to work by the organization thus

[32] Debates of the Constitutional Convention of Pennsylvania, 1873, v. 3, pp.
522-3.

spontaneously formed by the people. A complete embargo was placed on sales of oil at any price to the men who had made the hateful bargain with the railroads. The oil country was divided into sixteen districts, in each of which the producers elected a local committee, and over all these was an executive committee composed of representatives from the local committees—one from each. No oil was sold to be used within any district except to those buyers whom the local committee recommended; no oil was sold to be exported or refined outside the district, except to such buyers as the executive committee permitted. One cent a barrel was paid by each producer into a general fund for the expenses of the organization.

Steps were taken to form a company with a capital of $1,000,000, subscribed by the producers, to advance money, on the security of their oil, to those producers who did not want to sell.

Able lawyers were employed and sent with the committees to all the important capitals—Harrisburg, Washington, the offices of the railway companies. The flow of oil was checked, the activities of the oil world brought near a stop.

Monday, March 15th, by the influence of the Washington committee, a resolution was introduced into the House of Representatives by Representative Scofield, ordering an investigation of the South Improvement Company. Immediately upon this the frightened participants cancelled the contracts. By the 26th of March the representatives of the people had secured a pledge in writing from the five great railroads concerned of "perfect equality," and "no rebates, drawbacks, or other arrangements," in favor of any one thereafter. March 30th, Congress began the investigation which brought to light the evidence of the contracts, and meanwhile the committees on legislation and pipe lines were securing from the Pennsylvania Legislature the repeal of the South Improvement Company charter, and the passage of a "so-called" Free Pipe Line law, discovered afterwards to be worthless on account of amendments shrewdly inserted by the enemy.

The committee of Congress noticed when the contracts were afterwards shown to it, that though they had been so widely declared to be "cancelled," they had not been cancelled, but were as fresh—seals, stamps, signatures and all—as the day they were made. This little circumstance is descriptive of the whole proceeding. Both parties to this scheme to give the use of the highways as a privilege to a few, and through this privilege to make the pursuit of livelihood a privilege, theirs exclusively—the railroad officials on one side, and their beneficiaries of the South Improvement Company on the other—were resolute in their determination to carry out their purpose. All that follows of this story is but the recital of the sleuth-like tenacity with which this trail of fabulous wealth has been followed.

The chorus of cancellation from the railroads came from those who had meant never to cancel, really. In their negotiations with the representatives of the people they had contested to the last the abandonment of the scheme. "Their friendliness" to it "was so apparent," the Committee of the Producers reported, "that we could expect little consideration at their hands," [33] and the committee became satisfied that the railroads had made a new contract among themselves like that of the South Improvement Company, and to take its place. Its head frankly avowed before the Investigating Committee of Congress their intention of going ahead with the plan. "They are all convinced that, sooner or later, it will be necessary to organize upon the basis on which the South Improvement Company was organized, including both producers and refiners.".

This conviction has been faithfully lived up to. Under the name of the South Improvement Company the arrangement was ostentatiously abandoned, because to persist in it meant civil war in the oil country as the rising young anti-monopolist lawyer pointed out in the Constitutional Convention. Mark Twain, in describing the labors of the missionaries in the Sandwich Islands, says they were so successful that the vices of the natives no longer exist in name—only in reality. As every page will show, this contract no longer exists in name—only in reality. In the oil world, and in every other important department of our industrial life—in food, fuel, shelter, clothing, transportation,[34] this contract, in its various new shapes, has been kept steadily at work gerrymandering the livelihoods of the people.

The men who had organized the South Improvement Company paid the public revolt the deference of denial, though not of desistance. The company had got a charter, organized under it, collected twenty per cent. of the subscription for stock, made contracts with the railroads, held meetings of the directors, who ap-

[33] Report of Executive Committee of the Petroleum Producers' Union, 1872.
[34] See ch. xxxiii.

proved of the contracts and had received the benefits of the increase of freights made in pursuance of the agreement. This was
shown by the testimony of its own officers.[35]

But "the company never did a dollar's worth of business," the
Secretary of the Light of the World told Congress,[36] and "there was
never the slightest connection between the South Improvement
Company and the Standard Oil Company," the president of the
latter and the principal member of both said in an interview in
the New York *World*, of March 29, 1890. "The South Improvement Company died in embryo. It was never completely organized,
and never did any business. It was partly born, died, and was
buried in 1872," etc.

Still later, before a committee of the Legislature of New York
in 1888, he was asked about "the Southern Improvement Company."

"There was such a company?"

"I have heard of such a company."

"Were you not in it?"

"I was not." [37]

So help me God!

At almost the moment of this denial in New York, an associate
in this and all his other kindred enterprises, asked before Congress who made up the South Improvement Company, named as
among them the principal members of the great oil company, and
most conspicuous of them all was the name of this denier.[38]

The efficiency with which this "partly born" innocent lived his
little hour, "not doing a dollar's worth of business," was told in
a summary phrase by one of the managers of the Pennsylvania
Railroad, describing the condition of the oil business in 1873:[39]

"All other of our largest customers had failed."

When the people of the oil regions made peace after their uprising it was, as they say, with "full assurance from the Washington
committee that the throwing off the restrictions from trade will
not embarrass their investigation (by Congress), but that the Sub-
Committee of Commerce will, nevertheless, continue, as the princi-

[35] Report Executive Committee Petroleum Producers' Union, 1872.
[36] Trusts, Congress, 1888, p. 290.
[37] Testimony, Trusts, New York Senate, 1888, p. 420.
[38] Testimony, Trusts, Congress, 1888, p. 289.
[39] Testimony, Commonwealth of Pennsylvania *vs.* Pennsylvania Railroad Company *et al.*, 1879, p. 707.

ple involved, and not this particular case alone, is the object of
the investigation." [40]

The Committee of Commerce did not "continue." The principal
witness, who had negotiated the contracts by which the railroads
gave over the business of the oil regions to a few, refused in effect,
beyond producing copies of the contract, to be a witness. Permission was given by the Committee of Congress during its first zeal
to the Committee of Producers from Pennsylvania to copy the
testimony as it was taken, but no official record of its discoveries
exists. This transcript was published by the producers, and copies
are possessed by a few fortunate collectors. The committee did
not report, and in the aichives of the national Capitol no scrap
of the evidence taken is to be found. All has vanished into the
bottomless darkness in which the monopoly of light loves to dwell.

[40] Report Executive Committee Petroleum Producers' Union, 1872.

VIII

"No!"

There has never been any real break in the plans revealed, "partly born," "and buried" in 1872. From then till now, in 1893, every fact that has come to the surface has shown them in full career. If they were buried, it was as seed is—for a larger crop of the same thing.

The people had made peace, in 1872, on the pledge of "perfect equality" on the highways. Hardly had they got back to their work when they began to feel the pinch of privilege again. The Pennsylvania road alone is credited with any attempt to keep faith, and that only "for some months." "Gradually," as a committee of the people wrote to the managers of the Pennsylvania Railroad, "the persons constituting the South Improvement Company were placed by the roads in as favorable a position as to rates and facilities as had been stipulated in the original contract with that company." [1]

As soon as pipe lines were proved practicable they were built as rapidly as pipes and men to put them in the ground could be had, but there was some lubricant by which they kept constantly slipping into bankruptcy.

They were "frozen out," as one of their builders said, "summer as well as winter."

By 1874, twenty pipe lines had been laid in the oil country. Eighty per cent. of them died off in that and the following year.[2] The mere pipes did not die, they are there yet; but the ownership of the many who had built them died.

There were conservatives in the field to whom competition was

[1] Trusts, Congress, 1888, p. 363.
[2] Testimony, New York Assembly "Hepburn" Report, 1879, p. 1693.

as distasteful as to the socialists. To "overcome such competition," and to insure them "a full and regular" and "remunerative business" in pipe lines, in the language of the South Improvement Company contract, all that was needed was to put into operation the machinery of that contract which no longer existed—in name. The decease of the name was not an insuperable obstacle.

In exact reproduction of the plan of 1872, the railroads, in October, 1874, advanced rates to the general ruin, but to the pool of lines owned by their old friends of the South Improvement Company they paid back a large rebate. That those who had such a railroad Lord Bountiful to fill their pockets should grow rich fast was a matter of course.[3]

Getting this refund they got all the business. Oil, like other things, follows the line of least resistance, and will not flow through pipes where it has to pay when it can run free and get something to boot. Nobody could afford to buy oil except those who were in this deal. They could go into the market, and out of these bonuses could bid higher than any one else. They "could overbid in the producing regions, and undersell in the markets of the world." [4]

This was not all. In the circular which announced the bounty to the pet pipes there was another surprise. It showed that the roads had agreed to carry crude oil to their friends' refineries at Pittsburg and Cleveland without charge from the wells, and to charge them no more for carrying back refined oil to the seaboard for export than was charged to refineries next door to the wells and hundreds of miles nearer the market. "Outside" refiners who had put themselves near the wells and the seaboard were to be denied the benefit of their business sagacity. The Cleveland refiners, whose location was superior only for the Western trade, were to be forced into a position of unnatural equality in the foreign trade. In short, the railroads undertook to pay, instead of being paid, for what they carried for these friends, and force them into an equality with manufacturers who had builded better than they.

Evidently they who had contrived all this had their despondent moments, when they feared that its full beneficence would not be understood by a public unfamiliar with the "science of transportation."

To the new rules was attached an explanation which asserted the right of the railroads to prevent persons and localities from

[3] Rutter Circular, Trusts, Congress, 1888, p. 363.
[4] New York Assembly "Hepburn" Report, 1879, p. 44.

enjoying the advantage of any facility they may possess, no matter how "real."

"You will observe that under this system the rate is even and fair to all parties, preventing one locality taking advantage of its neighbor by reason of some alleged or real facility it may possess." [5]

Meanwhile good society was shuddering at its reformers, and declaring that they meant to stop competition and "divide up property."

"Do you do that in any business except oil?" the most distinguished railroad man of that day was asked. "Do you carry a raw product to a place 150 miles distant and back again to another point like that without charge, so as to put them on an equality?"

To which he replied—it was he who could not remember that he had ever seen the South Improvement Company contract he signed in 1872—"I don't know." [6]

"Could any more flagrant violation of every principle of railroad economy and natural justice be imagined than this?" the report of the New York Legislature asks.[7]

An expert introduced by the railroads defended this arrangement. He insisted that all pipe lines had a chance to enter the pool and get the same refund.[8] But a witness from the pipe-line country, who was brought to New York to testify to the relations of the railroads and the oil combination, let out the truth.

"Why didn't they go into the pool?" he was asked, in reference to one of the most important pipe lines.

"Because they were not allowed to. They wanted to freeze them out. They were shut out from the market practically." [9]

For these enterprises, as they failed one after the other, there was but one buyer—the group of gentlemen who called themselves the South Improvement Company in 1872, but now in the field of pipe-line activity had taken the name of United Pipe Line, since known as the National Transit Company, and then and now a part of the oil trust.

"The United Pipe Line bought up the pipes as they became bankrupt one after another," testified the same friendly witness.[10]

Then came a great railroad war in 1877. A fierce onslaught was

---

[5] Rutter Circular, Trusts, Congress, 1888, p. 363.
[6] Testimony, New York Assembly "Hepburn" Report, 1879, p. 1596.
[7] Ibid., Report, p. 43.
[8] Ibid., Testimony, p. 3429.
[9] Testimony, New York Assembly "Hepburn" Report, 1879, pp. 2792-95.
[10] Ibid., p. 2795.

made on the Pennsylvania Railroad by all the other trunk lines.
In this affair, as in all dynastic wars, the public knew really
nothing about what was being done or why. The newspapers were
filled with the smoke of the battles of the railroad kings; but the
newspapers did not tell, for they did not then know, that the railroads were but tools of conquest in the hands of greater men.

The cause of the trouble was that the managers of the Pennsylvania Railroad had begun to reach out for the control of the
oil trade. They had joined in the agreement in 1872 to give it to
the oil combination, but now they wanted it for themselves.
Through a mistletoe corporation—the Empire Transportation Company—they set to work building up a great business in oil cars,
pipe lines, refineries.

"We like competition; we like our competitors; we are neighbors
and friends, and have been all these years," the president of the
oil trust testified to the New York Legislature,[11] but he served
notice upon this competitor to abandon the field.[12] He and his associates determined to do more than compel the great railroad to
cease its competition. They determined to possess themselves of its
entire oil outfit, though it was the greatest corporation then in
America. This, the boldest stroke yet attempted, could be done
only with the help of the other trunk lines, and that was got.

The ruling officials of the New York Central, the Erie, the Baltimore and Ohio, the Lehigh Valley, the Reading, the Atlantic and
Great Western, the Lake Shore railroads, and their connections,
were made to believe, or pretended to believe, that it was their
duty to make an attack upon the Pennsylvania Railroad to force
it to surrender.[13] "A demand," says the New York Legislative Committee of 1879, "which they"—the railroads—"joined hands with
the Standard Oil Company and proceeded to enforce by a war of
rates, which terminated successfully in October of that year"
(1877).[14]

The war was very bitter. Oil was carried at eight cents a barrel
less than nothing by the Pennsylvania.[15] How low the rates were
made by the railroads on the other side is not known. The Penn-

[11] Testimony, Trusts, New York Senate, 1888, p. 445.
[12] Testimony, Commonwealth of Pennsylvania vs. Pennsylvania Railroad, et al.,
1879, p. 670.
[13] Testimony of A. J. Cassatt, Commonwealth of Pennsylvania vs. Pennsylvania
Railroad et al., 1879, pp. 666, 669, 671.
[14] New York Assembly "Hepburn" Report, 1879, p. 44.
[15] Testimony, Commonwealth of Pennsylvania, etc., 1879, p. 665.

sylvania was the first to sue for peace. Twice its vice-president "went to Canossa," which was Cleveland. It got peace and absolution only by selling its refineries and pipe lines and mortgaging its oil-cars to the oil combination. It "was left without the control of a foot of pipe line to gather, a tank to receive, or a still to refine a barrel of petroleum, and without the ability to secure the transportation of one, except at the will of men who live and whose interests lie in Ohio and New York." [16]

It was only seven years since the buyers had organized with a capital of $1,000,000. Now they were able to give their check for over $3,000,000 for this one purchase. "I was surprised," said Mr. Vanderbilt to the New York Legislative Committee of 1878, speaking of this transaction, "at the amount of ready cash they were able to provide." They secured, in addition to the valuable pipe lines, oil cars, and refineries in New York and Pennsylvania, the more valuable pledge given by the Pennsylvania Railroad that it would never again enter the field of competition in refining, and also a contract giving the oil combination one-tenth of all the oil freights received by the Pennsylvania Railroad, whether from the combination or its competitors—an arrangement it succeeded in making as well with the New York Central, Lake Shore, and other railroads.[17]

One of the earliest members of the oil combination was present at the meeting to consummate this purchase. Something over $3,000,000 of his and his associates' cash changed hands. The meeting was important enough to command the presence of a brigade of lawyers for the great corporations, and of the president, vice-president, and several directors of the Pennsylvania Railroad, and, representing the Poor Man's Light, the vice-president, the secretary, and five of the leading members of the combination, besides himself.[18]

But when asked in court about it he could not remember any such meeting. Finally, he recalled "being at a meeting," but he could not remember when it was, or who was there, or what it was for, or whether any money was paid.[19]

Three years later this transaction having been quoted against

[16] Appeal to the Executive of Pennsylvania, Trusts, Congress, 1888, p. 354.
[17] Testimony, Commonwealth of Pennsylvania vs. Pennsylvania Railroad et al., 1879, p. 735.
[18] Ibid., p. 672.
[19] Ibid., p. 460.

the combination in a way likely to affect the decision of a case in court, the treasurer denied it likewise. "It is not true as stated . . . directly or indirectly. . . ." [20]

Eight years later, when the exigencies of this suit of 1880, in Cleveland, had passed away, and a new exigency demanded a "revised version," the secretary of the combination told Congress that it was true. [21]

"The pleasures of memory," are evidently for poets, not for such millionaires. That appears to be the only indulgence they cannot afford.

The managers of the Pennsylvania road went back with the zeal of backsliders reconverted to their yoke in the service of the men who had given them this terrific whipping. They sent word to the independent refiners, whom they had secured as shippers by the pledge of 1872 of equal treatment, that equal rates and facilities could be given no longer. The producers and refiners did not sit down dumb under the death sentence. They begged for audience of their masters, masters of them because masters of the highway.

The third vice-president, the official in charge of the freight business, was sent to meet them.

"As you know," they began by reminding him, "we have been for the past year the largest shippers of petroleum the Pennsylvania Railroad has had."

He acknowledged it.

"Shall we, after the 1st of May, have as low a rate of freight as anybody else?" they then asked.

"No," he said; "after the 1st of May we shall give the Standard Oil Company lower rates than to you."

"How much discrimination will we have to submit to?" the poor "outsiders" asked.

"I decline to tell you," was the reply.

"How much business must we bring your road to get as good rates as the combination?" they then asked, and again—

"I decline to tell you," was the only answer they got.

"If we will ship as much, will you give us as low freight rates?"

"No."

"We have been shipping over the Pennsylvania Railroad a year," they persisted, "why can we not continue?"

[20] Standard Oil Company vs. W. C. Scofield et al. Affidavit of the treasurer of the Standard.
[21] Testimony, Trusts, Congress, 1888, pp. 771-72.

"It would make them mad; they are the only people who can make peace between the railroads."

"I think," said he, "you ought to fix it up with them. I am going over there this afternoon to talk with those people about this matter, and," he continued, "you will all be happy, and everything will work along very smoothly."

"We gave him very distinctly to understand that we did not propose to enter into any 'fix up' where we would lose our identity, or sell out, or be under anybody else's thumb; we are willing to pay as high a rate of freight as anybody, and we want it as low as anybody has it," they told him.

But the reply to all of it was, "You cannot have the same rate of freight."

As the magnate of the railroad seemed to be determined not to permit them to move to market along his rails, one of the independents referred to a plan for a new pipe line under consideration by them, the Equitable, as perhaps promising them the relief he refused.

"Lay all the pipe lines you like," the vice-president retorted, with feeling, "and we will buy them up for old iron."

The independents appealed from the third vice-president to the president; they had to beg repeatedly for a hearing before they got it. They came together in the June following, the independents coming on from New York for the purpose. Since their interview with the third vice-president rates had been advanced upon them, and not only that, but when they had oil ready to ship at those high freight rates, the railroad on one pretext or another refused them cars. One of them had contracts to deliver oil from his refinery in New York to go abroad. When he ordered the cars that were needed to take the crude oil to New York to be refined they were refused him. The ships lay idle at the docks, charging him heavy damages for every day of delay; at the wells his oil was running on the ground.

"You had better go and arrange with the Standard Oil Company; I don't want to get into any trouble with them," the president said. "If you are business men, you will make an arrangement with them. I will do all in my power to bring it about."

"We will never take our freight rates from them," they replied; "we are not willing to enter into any such arrangement."

"Why don't you go to the other roads?" the president asked his suppliants.

"We have done so. It's of no use. On the New York Central the cars are owned by the combination, and the Erie is in a like position. We have been shippers on the Pennsylvania Railroad a long, long while, and you ought to take care of us and give us all the cars we need. We are suffering very greatly for the want of them. Can we have the same rate that other shippers get?"

"No."

"If we ship the same amount of oil?"

"No."

"If you have not cars enough, will you, if we build cars, haul them?"

"No. You will not have any peace or prosperity," continued the president, "until you make terms with the combination."

Like the third vice-president he offered to intercede with them to get transportation over his own road for his own customers. Like men they refused the offer.

"We were, of course, very indignant," one of them said, in relating this experience in court.[22]

A little later a rich and expert refiner, who had sold out in 1876, made up his mind to try again. The Pennsylvania road had a new president by this time, but the old "no" was still in force.

"When I was compelled to succumb I thought it was only temporarily, that the time would come when I could go into the business I was devoted to. I was in love with the business. I took a run across the water; I was tired and discouraged and used up in 1878, and was gone three or four months. I came back ready for work, and had the plan, specifications and estimates made for a refinery that would handle ten thousand barrels of oil in a day. I selected a site near three railroads and a river; I would have spent about five hundred thousand dollars, and probably a couple of hundred thousand more. I believed the time had arrived when the Pennsylvania Railroad would see their true interest as common carriers, and the interest of their stockholders, and the business interest of the City of Philadelphia. I called on the President of the Pennsylvania Railroad; I laid the plans before him, and told him I wanted to build a refinery of ten thousand barrels' capacity a day. I was almost on my knees begging him to allow me to do that.

[22] For the full report of these remarkable interviews with the President and Third Vice-President of the Pennsylvania Railroad see Testimony, Investigation Pennsylvania Secretary of Internal Affairs, 1878, pp. 47 et seq., 60 et seq.; Testimony, Commonwealth of Pennsylvania vs. Pennsylvania Railroad et al., 1879, pp. 160 et seq., 204 et seq., 237 et seq.

" 'What is it you want?' he said.

" 'Simply to be put upon an equality with everybody else—especially the Standard Oil Company. I want you to agree with me that you will give me transportation of crude oil as low as you give it to anybody else for ten years, and then I will give you a written assurance that I will do this refining of ten thousand barrels of oil a day for ten years. Is not that an honest position for us to be in? I as a manufacturer, you the president of a railroad.'

" 'I cannot go into any such agreement.'

"I saw the third vice-president. He said, in his frank way, 'That is not practicable, and you know the reason why.' " [23]

After their interviews with the President and Vice-President of the Pennsylvania Railroad, these outsiders went to the officials of the other roads, only to hear the same "No!" from all.[24]

At one time, to get oil to carry out their contracts and fill the vessels which were waiting at the docks and charging them damages for the delay, these refiners telegraphed to the oil regions offering the producers there ten cents above the market price if they could get oil to them over any of the roads to New York. They answered they could not get the cars, and none of them accepted the offer.[25]

All the roads—as in 1872—were in league to "overcome" them.

Thus, at a time when the entire movement of oil was at the rate of only 25,000 or 30,000 barrels a day, and the roads had cars enough to move 60,000 barrels a day, these independent refiners found themselves shut completely off from the highway.[26] The Pennsylvania Railroad, the New York Central, the Erie, and their branches and connections in and out of the oil regions, east and west, were as entirely closed to them as if a foreign enemy had seized the country and laid an embargo on their business—which was, indeed, just what had happened. The only difference between that kind of invasion and what had really come was, that "the dear people," as the president of the trust called them,[27] would have known they were in the hands of an enemy if he had come beating his drums loud enough, and firing off his two-thousand

[23] Testimony, Trusts, Congress, 1888, pp. 225-26.
[24] Testimony, Investigation, Pennsylvania Secretary of Internal Affairs, 1878, pp. 49, 59; Testimony, New York Assembly "Hepburn" Report, 1879, pp. 710, 3548-56; Exhibits, ibid., p. 176; Testimony, Commonwealth of Pennsylvania vs. Pennsylvania Railroad et al., 1879, p. 247.
[25] Testimony, New York Assembly "Hepburn" Report, p. 712.
[26] Ibid., p. 720.
[27] Testimony, Trusts, New York Senate, 1888, p. 445.

pounders often enough, and pricking them deep enough with his bayonets; but their wits are not yet up to knowing him when he comes among them disguised as an American citizen, although they see property destroyed and life lost and liberty thrown wherever he moves.

There was enough virtue in Pennsylvania to begin a suit in the name of the State against the men who were using its franchises for such purposes, though there was not enough to push it to a decision. The Third Vice-President of the Pennsylvania Railroad, when examined as a witness in this suit, confirmed these statements about the interviews with himself and the president of the road in every particular about which he was questioned.

"We stated to the outside refiners that we would make lower rates to the Standard Oil Company than they got; we declined to allow them to put cars of their own on the road." [28]

His evidence fills seventy-six pages, closely printed, in the report of testimony. It was clear, full, and candid; remarkably so, considering that it supplied officially from the company's own records the facts, item by item, which proved that the management of the Pennsylvania Railroad had violated the Constitution of Pennsylvania and the common law, and had taken many millions of dollars from the people and from the corporation which employed them, and secretly, and for no consideration, had given them to strangers.

The railway officials are, in the world of the highway, the government. They hold their supreme power to tax commerce, and to open and close the highways, solely and altogether by grant of the State, and under the law of the common carrier. It is only by the exercise of the sovereign power to eminent domain to take the property of a private individual by force, without his consent, for public use—never for any other than public use—and only by the grant of the right to cross city streets and country roads that the railroads come into existence at all. This says nothing of the actual cash given to the railroad projectors by the government, which, in New York State alone, amounts to upwards of $40,000,000.[29]

The independent refiners represent the people, claiming of the highway department of their government those equal rights which all citizens have as a birthright, and the government informs these

[28] Testimony, Commonwealth of Pennsylvania vs. Pennsylvania Railroad et al., 1879, pp. 725-26.
[29] Exhibits, New York Assembly "Hepburn" Report, 1879, pp. 238-45.

citizens that their rights on the highways have been given as a private estate to certain friends of the ruling administration, much as William the Conqueror would give this rich abbey or that fertile manor to one of his pets.

"We have no franchise that is not open to all," say the "trustees." "It is a free open market." "There is nothing peculiar to our companies." "It is as free as air."

In truth they have had no less a franchise than, as in 1872, the excluding possession of all the great trunk-lines out of the oil country, and all their connections east and west, and this franchise has since widened until, in 1893, it reaches from ocean to ocean, and from gulf to gulf.

Their franchise was meant to be as exclusive as if they had had from the government letters-patent in the old royal fashion of close monopolies in East Indian trade, or salt, or tobacco at home, giving them by name the sole right to use the roads, and forbidding all others, under pain of business death, from setting their foot on the highway. But with this difference: the exclusive franchise in the latter case would exist by law; but in this case it was created in defiance of law, exists in contempt of the law, and in its living the law dies daily.

The refiners and producers who were pleading in this way with the railroads for a chance to live after May 1, never doubted but that, as they were told, and as their arrangements with the Pennsylvania road guaranteed, they were having and were to have at worst until that date, equal and impartial rates and facilities. Under this safe-conduct they parleyed for the future. But the Pennsylvania Railroad was at that moment negotiating with the oil combination to collect from the independents, under the guise of freight, 20 to 22½ cents a barrel on all they sent to market, and pay it over to the combination. The payments were made to one of the rings within the oil ring, called the American Transfer Company. "It is the same instrumentality under a different name," said the counsel of the New York Chamber of Commerce before the New York Legislature. The official of the Pennsylvania road who issued the order to take this money out of the treasury pleaded in excuse that proof had been given him that other roads were doing the same thing.[30] Receipted bills were brought to him, showing that the New York Central and the Erie had been "for many months" paying these men who called themselves American Transfer Company

[30] New York Assembly "Hepburn" Report, 1879, Exhibits, pp. 479-514.

for having "protected" their oil business, sums ranging from 20 cents to 35 cents a barrel on all the oil those roads transported.[31] So deeply was the watch-dog of the Pennsylvania road's treasury affected by the proof that his company was doing less than the other roads, that he instructed the comptroller to give these men three months' back pay, which was done. Twenty cents a barrel was sent them out of all the oil freights collected by the Pennsylvania for the three months preceding, and thereafter the tribute was paid them monthly. Then it was increased to 22½ cents a barrel. The same amount per barrel was refunded to them out of their own freight. They received this on all oil shipped by them, and also on all shipped by their competitors.[32] They who received this tribute pretended to the railroad officials that they "protected" the roads from losing business. The railroad men pretended to believe it.

The way in which this revenue was given and got shows what a simple and easy thing modern business really is—not in any way the brain-racker political economists have persuaded themselves and us. The representative of the oil combination writes a bright, cheery letter; the representative of the Pennsylvania answers it, and there you are; 22½ cents a barrel on millions of barrels flows out of the cash-box of the railroad into the cash-box of the combination. In one year, 1878, this tribute, at the rate of 22½ cents on the 13,750,-000 barrels of oil shipped by the three trunklines, must have amounted to $3,093,750. The American Transfer Company had a little capital of $100,000, and its receipts from this rebate in this one year would amount to dividends of 3093 per cent. annually; the capital of the oil combination which owned this Transfer Company was at this time $3,500,000.

There are reasons to believe that some of the very railroad men who turned the money of the railroads over to the American Transfer Company were among its members. But if all the profit went to the combination, and none of it was for the railway officials through whom they got it, their revenue from that source alone would have paid in 1878 a dividend nearly equal to this capital of

[31] This was always denied by the New York Central. "I never heard of the American Transfer Company," Vanderbilt told the New York Legislature. "I don't know that we ever paid the American Transfer Company a dollar. If we did, I have no knowledge of it." New York Assembly "Hepburn" Report, 1879, p. 1577.

[32] Testimony, Commonwealth of Pennsylvania vs. Pennsylvania Railroad et al., p. 702. Ibid., Exhibits Nos. 45-47, pp. 732-33.

$3,500,000. In this device of the American Transfer Company we again see reappear in 1878, in high working vitality, the supposed corpse of the South Improvement Company of 1872. The American Transfer Company was ostensibly a pipe line, and the railroad officials met the exposure of their "nothing peculiar" dealings with it by asserting that the payment to it of 22½ cents a barrel and more was for its service in collecting oil and delivering it to them; but the Third Vice-President of the Pennsylvania Railroad admits that his road paid the money on oil which the American Transfer Company never handled.

"This 22½ cents (a barrel) paid the American Transfer Company is not restricted to oil that passed through their lines?"

"No, sir; it is paid on all oil received and transported by us." [33]

The American Transfer Company was not even a pipe line. By the Pennsylvania laws all incorporated pipe lines must report their operations and condition monthly to the State. But the publisher of the petroleum trade reports, and organizer of a bureau of information about petroleum, with offices in Oil City, London, and New York, issuing daily reports, testified that the American Transfer Company was not known in the oil regions at all as a pipe line. It published none of the statements required by law. "They do not," he said, "make any runs from the oilwells." It had once been a pipe line, but "years ago it was merged in with other lines," and consolidated into the United Pipe Line, owned and operated by the combination.[34]

When this arrangement was exposed to public view by the New York legislative investigation, the "expert" who appeared to explain it away in behalf of the railroads and their beneficiaries, paraded a false map of the pipe-line system, drawn and colored to make it seem that the American Transfer Company was a very important pipe-line.[35] This was the same "expert" who, as we saw, defended the pipe-line holocaust of 1874 by asserting that "all were to be taken in alike."

The New York Legislature found, in 1879, that the oil combination thus owned and controlled the oil terminal facilities of the four trunklines at New York, Philadelphia, and Baltimore.

"They can use the power here given, and have used it to crush out opposition." [36]

[33] Commonwealth of Pennsylvania *vs.* Pennsylvania Railroad *et al.*, 1879, p. 691.
[34] Testimony, New York Assembly "Hepburn" Report, 1879, pp. 3666-69.
[35] *Ibid.*, p. 3959.
[36] New York Assembly "Hepburn" Report, 1879, pp. 40-44.

"Of course, there is in the Erie contract a statement that every shipper of oil over the road shall be treated with 'fairness' by the Standard Oil Company, and our attention was drawn to that," the counsel of the Chamber of Commerce said. . . . "In the first place, they have the exclusive shipment of oil, and therefore nobody could ship oil, and there was no oil handled for anybody else; but if the Erie Company should send some for somebody else, why, the sloop could not get to the dock, and the machinery at the dock would not and could not work by any possibility so as to get that oil out of that dock and into a ship (except at the end of a lawsuit)." [37]

Evidently the "cancellation" of 1872 had not cancelled anything of substance. Indeed, the "no" of 1878 was wider than the embargo of 1872, for the fourth great trunk-line, the Baltimore and Ohio, was not one of the signatories then; by 1878 it had, like all the others, closed its port to the people—farming it out as the old regime farmed out the right to tax provinces.

He used to meet the president of the oil combination "frequently in the Erie office," a friend and subordinate has recalled.[38] Railroad offices are pleasant places to visit when such plums are to be gathered there as this of the sole right to the freedom of all ports and control of the commerce of three continents.

Down to this writing, when the little group of independents who remain masters of their own refineries along Oil Creek seek to send their oil in bulk abroad, or to transship it at any one of the principal ports for other points on the coast, the same power still says the same "no" as twenty years ago.[39]

[37] Speech of Simon Sterne, counsel of the New York Chamber of Commerce, before New York Assembly "Hepburn" Committee, 1879, p. 3964.
[38] *Ibid.*, Testimony, p. 2772.
[39] See ch. xi.

IX

Who Piped and Who Danced

Thus, by 1878, the independent producers and refiners found themselves caught in a battue like rabbits driven in for the sport of a Prince of Wales.

If the richest person then in America—that artificial but very real person the Pennsylvania Railroad—could not keep its pipe lines, nobody could. The war for the union, which ended with its surrender in 1877, closed the pipe-line industry to the people. The unanimous "no" of all the railroads which followed completed the corral.

Oil, when it got to market, found that those who had become the owners of the pipe lines were also the owners of most of the refineries, and so the only large buyers.[1] "Practically to-day there is but one buyer of crude oil for us. . . . We take our commodity to one buyer; we take the price he chooses to give us without redress, with no right of appeal."[2]

The producers were being ground to powder by the fact that an enemy had possession of their local pipes, their tankage, and their railways. "I am the unfortunate owner," said one of them, "of interests in nearly one hundred pumping wells. I have produced over half a million barrels of oil."[3] Oil was running out of the ground at the rate of 15,000,000 barrels a year, but the New York refiners who were in command of plenty of capital, said:

"We don't dare build large refineries, for we don't know where we could get the oil."[4]

At last the people organized the Tidewater Pipe Line. This was

---

[1] New York Assembly "Hepburn" Report, 1879, p. 44.
[2] Testimony, Commonwealth of Pennsylvania *vs.* Pennsylvania Railroad *et al.*, 1879, pp. 302, 314.
[3] *Ibid.*, p. 295.
[4] *Ibid.*, p. 212.

the first successful attempt to realize the idea often broached of a pipe line to the seaboard. It was the last hope of the "outsiders" —the "independents." "Nothing short of the ingenuity that is born of necessity and desperation" produced that pipe line. It was well contrived and well manned, and had plenty of money. It was organized in 1878, with a capital of $1,000,000, which increased in a few years to $5,000,000. It built a pipe from the oil regions to Williamsport—105 miles—on the Philadelphia and Reading Railroad, whence the oil was carried in cars by that company and over the Jersey Central to Philadelphia and New York.

Unlimited capital and strategy did all that could be done against the Tidewater. At one place, to head it off, a strip of land barring its progress was bought entirely across a valley. It escaped by climbing the hills. At another point it had to cross under a railroad. The railroad officers forbade. Riding around, almost in despair, its engineer saw a culvert where there was no watercourse. It was for a right of passage which a farmer, whose land was cut in two by the railroad, had reserved in perpetuity for driving his cattle in safety to pasture. It did not take long to make a bargain with the farmer for permission to lay the pipe there.

The pipe line was finished and ready to move oil about the 1st of June, 1879. On June 5th a meeting was held at Saratoga of representatives of the four trunk-line railroads and of members of the oil trust. The meeting decided that the new competitor should be fought to the death. The rate on oil, which had been $1.15 a barrel, was reduced to 80, then to 30, to 20, to 15 cents by the railroads, to make the business unprofitable enough to ruin this first attempt to pipe oil to the seaboard. Finally the roads carried a barrel, weighing 390 pounds, 400 miles for the combination for 10 cents or less.[5] The representative of the Tidewater offered to prove to Congress, in 1880, if it would order an investigation— which it would not—that "the announced and ostensible object of the conference at Saratoga was to destroy the credit of the Tidewater, and to enable the oil combination to buy up the new pipe line, and that a time was fixed by the combination within which it promised to secure the control of the pipe line—provided the trunk-lines would make the rates for carrying oil so low that all concerned in transportation would lose money.[6] "There can be no

[5] New York Assembly "Hepburn" Report, 1879, p. 45.
[6] Franklin B. Gowen, before House Committee of Commerce, Washington, Jan. 27, 1880.

doubt," he continued, "that, taking the avowed and ostensible object of the Saratoga meeting as the true one, it constituted, on the part of the willing participants, a criminal conspiracy of the most dangerous character."

One of the chief officials of the Pennsylvania Railroad testified to the competition which his road had carried on with the Tidewater. "It certainly was fought," he said; "the rates were considerably reduced." [7] Rates were put down to points so low that the railroad men would never tell what they were. I have no knowledge—I have no recollection—was all the president and general freight agent of the Pennsylvania Railroad could be got to say, when before the Interstate Commerce Commission.[8] "Not enough to pay for the wheel grease," said the general freight agent.[9] The oil trust also cut the prices of pipeage by its local lines from 20 cents to 5 cents a barrel, turning cheapness into the enemy of cheapness.

But the Tidewater was strong enough to withstand even so formidable an assault as this. As its business was small, its losses were small; but the railroads, making this war on it for the benefit of others, suffered heavily. The trunk-lines, it has been calculated, wilfully threw away profits equal to $10,000,000 a year for the sake of inflicting a loss of $100,000 on the pipe lines.[10] Enough revenue was lost to pay dividends of 2½ to 5 per cent. on the total capital of the roads.

The customers of the Tidewater, the independent refiners in Philadelphia, were charged by the Pennsylvania Railroad on oil that came through the Tidewater 15 cents a barrel for one mile of hauling. The utmost the law allowed them was half a cent a mile, and they were carrying oil 500 miles to New York for the same charge of 15 cents a barrel, and less. Under such pressure these independent refineries, which the Tidewater had been built to supply, sold out one after another. The Tidewater was then in the position of a great transporting company, that had spent a large amount of money to bring a great product to its Philadelphia terminus, and found that refining establishments which had been begging it to give them oil had become the cohorts of its opponent.

[7] Testimony, Titusville and Oil City Independents' cases, before Interstate Commerce Commission, pp. 299-300.

[8] *Ibid.*, pp. 521, 539.

[9] *Ibid.*, p. 534.

[10] Franklin B. Gowen, before House Committee of Commerce, Washington, Jan. 27, 1880.

To meet this the Tidewater built refineries of its own at Chester, and at Bayonne, New Jersey, on New York waters. When asked for a rate to another point, the Pennsylvania gave one that was three and four times as much as they would charge the oil trust, but added, "we cannot make a rate on the empty cars returning." That is, as it was interpreted, "we will carry the oil, but we will not permit the empty cars to come over the roads to get the oil. They must be taken on a wheelbarrow, or by canal, or by balloon." [11] The war went on. Attempts were made to seduce the officials of the Tidewater. A stockholder, who had been too poor to pay for his stock, received a large sum from the oil combination and began a vexatious suit for a receivership.[12] A minority forced their way into the offices of the company, and took violent possession of it by a "farcical, fraudulent, and void" election, as the court decided in annulling it. Its financial credit was attacked in the money market and by injunctions against its bonds.

Affidavits were offered from members of the oil combination denying that they had had anything to do with these proceedings. In reference to these affidavits, the representative of the Tidewater reminded the court that that combination was a multifarious body. "One-half of them," he said, "do a thing, and the other half swear they know nothing about it. In pursuance of this Machiavelian policy, they have eight or ten gentlemen to conduct negotiations, and eight or ten to say they do not know anything about them."

Then, with no visible cause, the capacity of the pipe fell below the demands upon it. This insufficient capacity was pleaded in court as one of the reasons why the pipe should be taken out of the hands of its owners. One day the cause was discovered—a plug of wood. Some mysterious hand had been set to drive a square block of wood into the pipe so as to cut down its capacity to one-third. The representative of the Tidewater declared in court his belief that this plug had been placed by "people on the other side who have made affidavits in this case." A similar deed, but much worse, as it might have cost many lives, was done during the contest with Toledo, nine years later.[13]

The Tidewater was successful, but not successful enough. It owned 400 miles of pipe, including the 105 miles of the trunk-line,

[11] Franklin B. Gowen, before Pennsylvania House of Representatives Committee on Railroads, Feb. 13, 1883.

[12] See ch. xiii.   [13] See ch. xxvi.

and had control of nearly 3,000,000 barrels of tankage. It did a
great work for the people. "It was," the Philadelphia *Press* said,
in 1883, "the child of war. It has been a barrier between the producers and the monopoly which would crush them if it dared."
While these words of exultation were being penned, a surrender
was under negotiation. The Tidewater's managers were nearly worn
out. These tactics of corrupting their officers, slandering their credit,
buying up their customers, stealing the elections, garroting them
with lawsuits founded on falsehoods, shutting them off the railroads, and plugging up their pipe in the dark, were too much.
They entered into a pool. The two companies in the summer of
1883 "recognized" each other, as the trunk lines do, and agreed
to divide the business in proportions, which would net the Tidewater $500,000 a year. The announcement that this pool had been
formed on the Tidewater fell like a death-blow on the people of
the oil regions. "The Tidewater," the Philadelphia *Press* said, editorially, "will probably retain a nominal identity as a corporation,
but its usefulness to the public and its claim to popular confidence
and encouragement were extinguished the instant it consented to
enter into alliance with the unscrupulous monopoly which resorts
to that means of conciliating and bribing what it had failed to
destroy."

The Interstate Commerce Commission in 1892 judicially found
the same fact. It says: "About December, 1883, the pipe lines, with
the view of getting better rates, adjusted their differences, and the
competition between them ceased. The pipe-line business appears
then to have passed into the control of the National Transit Company." [14] All but 6 per cent. of the National Transit Company is
owned by the oil trust. It formed practically one-third the impos-
ing bulk of the $70,000,000 of the trust of 1882.[15] If anything can
be made certain by human testimony this evidence proves that
these pipe lines stopped competing in 1883. The witnesses are the
men who negotiated the contract, and upon whose approval it de-
pended. But when the president of the trust was asked under oath,
in 1888, if there were any pipe lines to tide-water competing with
it, he named, as "a competing company," "the Tidewater Pipe
Line."

[14] Titusville and Oil City Independents' cases; Interstate Commerce Commission reports, vol. v., pp. 4, 5.
[15] Trusts, New York Senate, 1888, p. 572.

"The Tidewater Company? Does that compete with your company?"

"It does."

"It is in opposition to it?"

"It is in opposition to it." [16]

In the same spirit he denied, in 1883, that he had anything to do with the company which had represented the oil trust in this "swallowing or something" of the Tidewater, This, the National Transit Company, was the most important member of the trust. Under its cover, by means like those described, from New York to West Virginia and Ohio, almost all the pipes for gathering and distributing oil have been brought into one ownership. Millions yearly of the earnings of this company were pooled with all the others in the trust, and the president was receiving his share of them four times a year. He was the sole attorney[17] authorized to sign contracts for the trustees, who thus held all the combined companies in a common control. These trustees, of whom he was the chief, not only controlled but owned as their personal property more than half the stock of every company represented. But these facts were not then known to the public. It was not intended that they should be known, as the struggle to conceal them from the New York Legislature five years later—in 1888—showed.

"Have you any connection with the National Transit Company?" he was asked, after taking the oath.

"I have not." [18]

These oil men saw what the railroad men had not the wit to see —or else lacked the virtue to live up to—that the pipe line is an oil railway. It requires no cars and no locomotives; it moves oil without risk of fire or loss; it is very much cheaper than the ordinary railway, for this freight moves itself after being lifted up by pumps. The pipe line was the sure competitor of the railway, fated to be either its servant or master, as the railroad chose to use it or lose it. The railways sentimentally helped the trust to gather these rival transportation lines into its hands; then the trust, with the real genius of conquest, threw the railroads to one side. A system of trunk-line pipes was at once pushed vigorously to completion in all directions. While the members of the oil trust

[16] Trusts, New York Senate, 1888, pp. 389-99.
[17] Ibid., p. 658.
[18] Testimony, Corners, New York Senate, 1883, p. 925.

were building these pipe lines to take away the oil business of the
railroads, the officials of the latter were giving them by rebates
the money to do it with. At the expense of their own employers,
the owners of the railroads, these freight agents and general managers presented to the monopoly, out of the freight earnings of the
oil business, the money with which to build the pipe lines that
would destroy that branch of the business of the roads.

It was the Tidewater that proved the feasibility of trunk pipe
lines. The trunk pipe lines the combination has built were in
imitation. Extraordinary pains have been taken to sophisticate
public opinion with regard to all these matters—for the ignorance
of the public is the real capital of monopoly—and with great success. The history we have transcribed from the public records is
refined by one of the combination into the following illuminant:

"About 1879 or 1880 it was discovered that railways were inadequate to the task of getting oil to the seaboard as rapidly as needed.
Combined capital and energy were equal to the emergency. No
need to detail how it was done. To-day there reaches," [19] etc., etc.
It must have been on some such authority that this, from one of
our leading religious journals, was founded: "Only by such union"
—of the refiners—"could pipe lines have been laid from the oil
wells to the tide-water, reducing to the smallest amount the cost of
transportation." [20] An account of the pipe-line system in the New
York Sun, of December 14, 1887, describing the operations of the
great pumps that force the oil through the pipes, says: "Every time
the piston of the engine passes forward and back a barrel of oil is
sent seaward. A barrel of oil is forced on its way every seven
seconds of every hour of the twenty-four. Every pulsation of the
gigantic pumps that are throbbing ceaselessly day and night is
known and numbered at headquarters in New York at the close of
each day's business." This heart of a machine, beating at the headquarters in New York, and numbering its beats day and night,
stands for thousands of hearts whose throbs of hope have been
transmuted into this metallic substitute. This heart counts out a
gold dollar for every drop of blood that used to run through the
living breasts of the men who divined, projected, accomplished,
and lost.

It is impossible to compute how much the defeat of legislation
to regulate charges, or to allow the construction of competing lines,

[19] *Combinations*, S. C. T. Dodd, p. 28.
[20] New York *Independent*, March 17, 1893.

has cost the people. The Burdick Bill alone, to regulate prices of pipeage and storage in Pennsylvania, it was calculated by conservative men, would have saved at least $4,000,000 a year. The killing of it was in the interest of keeping up the high prices of the pipe lines, which finally rest in the price of oil.

When the combination got possession of the pipe line to Buffalo, which others had built in spite of every obstacle it could interpose, it raised the rates of pipeage to 25 cents a barrel from 10 cents,[21] and as happened in Pennsylvania in 1885, the railroads to Buffalo in 1882 raised their rates simultaneously with the pipe line. Pittsburg had the same experience. When its independent pipe line was "united and systemized" by being torn up and converted into "old iron," as the Vice-President of the Pennsylvania Railroad had told its projectors it would be, the rates of transportation for oil went up.[22] The same thing happened at Cleveland. At the rate at which the Lake Shore road carries oil from Cleveland to Chicago—357 miles for 38 cents a barrel—it should charge less than 15 cents for the 140 miles between Oil City and Cleveland; but as late as 1888 it charged 25 cents. Why? The effect of the railroad charge is that little oil comes by rail to Cleveland from the oil regions; it goes by the pipe line of those whom the Lake Shore has been "protecting" ever since the South Improvement contract of 1872. There have been 3,000,000 barrels of this business yearly. The railroad officials exercise their powers to drive traffic from the railroad to a competing line. Why? We can see why the combination, which, by the possession of this pipe line, is a competitor of the Lake Shore, should desire such an arrangement; but it exists by the act of the Lake Shore Railroad. Why? The theories of self-interest would lead one to expect that the stockholders of the road would find out why.

The pipe lines are the largest single item in the property of the oil combination. Here its control has been the most complete; and here the reduction of price has been least. This is a telltale fact, soon told and soon understood.

[21] Testimony, Trusts, Congress, 1888, p. 425.
[22] *The Railways and the Republic*, by J. F. Hudson, p. 83.

XI

Song of the Barrel

Genius could take so unspeakable a thing as a shirt and sing it into an immortal song, but a barrel—and an oil-barrel, greasy and ill-smelling—even genius could do nothing with that. But the barrel plays a leading role in the drama of the great monopoly. Out of it have flown shapes of evil that have infected private fortunes, the prosperity of more than one industry, the fiduciary honor of great men, the faithfulness of the Government to its citizens. Perhaps a part of what genius could do for the shirt—force a hearing for the wronged—may be done for this homely vessel of the struggling independent by the kindly solicitude of the people to learn every secret spring of the ruin of their brothers.

The market—the barrel that went to market—the freight rate that stopped the barrel that went to market—the railway king who made the rate that stopped the barrel that went to market—the greater king who whispered behind to the railway king to make the rate that stopped the barrel that went to market—this is the house that Jack unbuilt.

Such is the superiority of a simple business organization, where "evolution" has not carried the details of the industry out of sight of the owner, and where the master and man, buyer and seller, are in touch, that the independent refiners could overcome the tax imposed on them by this pooling of the pipe line and the railroads, and not only survive but prosper moderately. During the three years—from 1885 to 1888—following the first attack, they state, in their appeal to the Interstate Commerce Commission in 1888, they were "enabled by their advantages in the local markets to keep up,

52

maintain, and even increase their business." [1] These "outsiders" shipped their oil largely in barrels because the trunk-lines had made it as nearly impossible as they could for them to ship in tank-cars. They, like all in the trade, could not live without access to the European market. Out of every hundred barrels of various kinds of products from the distillation of petroleum, forty are of an illuminating oil not good enough to be burned in this country. It must be sold in Europe or not sold at all; and a manufacturer who cannot get rid of 40 per cent. of his product must give up manufacturing. To destroy the barrel method of shipment would destroy those who could use no other; and to close their outlet to Europe would make it impossible for them to continue to manufacture for the home supply. The barrel was the only life-raft left to the sinking independent.

They who had planned the secret pool of 1885 between the pipe line and the railroads, and the further advance of rates by both in 1888, now called upon the railroads to deliver a final stroke against the independents.[2] The railroads, when directed in previous years to say "no" to applications for transportation, and "no" to those who wanted the right to put their own tank-cars on the road, had obeyed; they obeyed again.

A pretext for the suppression of the barrel was easily found. It was a poor one, but poor pretexts are better than none. When the future "trustees" of the "light of the world" were doing a small fraction of the business, they got the contract of 1872 from the railroads to "overcome" all their competitors, on the pretext of "increasing the trade." [3] When by this contract and those that followed it they had secured nine-tenths of the trade, they got the railroads to say "no" to the remaining one-tenth, on the pretext that they could not ship as much.[4] When the Interstate Commerce law declared it to be a crime for railroads to forbid persons the road because they could not ship as much as others, the combination had the railroads shut out its rivals, on the pretext that they did not use tank-cars,[5] although tank-cars "are worse than powder."

[1] Titusville and Oil City Independents' cases, Nos. 153, 154, 163. Petition and Complaint, p. 4.
[2] Interstate Commerce Commission, "In the Matter of Relative Tank and Barrel Rates on Oil," 1888. Letter of G. B. Roberts.
[3] See ch. v.
[4] See ch. viii.
[5] See below, and ch. xvii.

When regular tank-cars were offered by its competitors for shipment
—as to the Pacific coast—the combination introduced an inferior
tank-car, of which it claimed, without warrant, as the courts afterwards held, that it owned the patent, and so obtained the sole right
of way across the continent, on the pretext that other shippers did
not use this poor car.[6]

The pretext now used against the refiners of Pennsylvania was
the passing phrase, "He must pay freight on barrels," in a decision
of the Interstate Commerce Commission concerning Southern traffic.
This decision had no relevancy to the oil business of the North.
Six months went by after it was given with no intimation from any
one that it related in any way to the situation in Pennsylvania,
and to be so applied it had to be turned inside out and upside
down. In the Rice case the Commission had decided that freight
rates must be reduced on barrel shipments. This was, in the sharp
language of the decision, to put an end to "the most unjust and
injurious discrimination against barrel shippers in favor of tank
shippers," a discrimination which the Commission has elsewhere
said "inured mostly to the benefit of one powerful combination."

In ordering this reduction it said: "Even then the shipper in
barrels is at some disadvantage, for he must pay freight on barrels
as well as on oil."

By "must pay" the Commission meant "was paying." It was, as
it afterwards protested, "rather a statement of a prevailing practice
than a ruling." [7] And the remark furthermore concerned the trade
in the South and Southwest alone, where special circumstances existed not found at the North.

Six months after this decision the Pennsylvania and other North-
ern roads made these words, "He must pay freight on the barrels,"
the occasion of an increase of rates, which stopped the refineries
of the independents. They were carrying free the heavy tanks—"the
most undesirable business we do," in the language of their freight
agent. They had been carrying the barrels of the independents free
for twenty years. Now, continuing to carry the tank-cars free, they
levied a prohibitory transportation tax on the barrels. To cap it
all, they declared, in announcing the new rule, that it had been
forced upon them by the Interstate Commerce Commission. But
the President of the Pennsylvania Railroad is found admitting
that it was the oil combination that dictated the move—"the sea-

---

[6] See ch. xxxiii.
[7] Rice, Robinson & Witherop case, Interstate Commerce Commission, 1890.

board refiners insisted." "Upon your decision" (in the Rice case) "being promulgated," he wrote the Interstate Commerce Commission, "the seaboard refiners insisted that we were bound to charge for packages," barrels, not tanks, "as well as for the oil." [8]

The seaboard refiners were the members of the oil trust; the others at the seaboard had been wiped out years before by the help of the railroads. Though the Pennsylvania Railroad was not a party to the case before the Commission, though it had not been called upon to change its practice, which was what it ought to be, it did now change it from right to wrong. The Commission had ordered that discrimination between the barrel and the tank should cease. The Pennsylvania, which had not, strange to say, been practising that forbidden kind of discrimination, immediately resorted to it, and, stranger still, gave as its reason the order of the Commission against it. It must have been a keen eye that could find in a "qualified and incidental remark," as the Interstate Commerce Commission styles it, in such a decision, a command to charge for the weight of the barrels and increase freight rates; but such an eye there was—an eye that will never sleep as long as Naboth's vineyard belongs to Naboth.

All the trunk-line railroads to the East took part in the new regulation—September 3, 1888—that freight must be paid thereafter on the weight of the barrels as well as on the oil itself, and at the same rate. This increased the cost of transportation to New York to 66 cents from 52 cents, and to other points proportionately. Freight rates on the oil of "the seaboard refiners" who shipped in tanks were left untouched. In the circulars announcing the change it was said to be done "in accordance with the directions of the Interstate Commerce Commission." [9] When the refiners whom this advance threatened with ruin wrote to expostulate, they got the same reply from all the railroad officials as from President Roberts of the Pennsylvania Railroad: "The advance in rates . . . has been forced upon us by the Interstate Commerce Commission." [10]

The Commission immediately called the responsible official of the Pennsylvania Railroad, which was the leader in this move, "to a personal interview," "expressed their surprise," and suggested the withdrawal of the circular and of the increased rates. This was

[8] In the matter of Relative Tank and Barrel Rates on Oil. Letter of President Roberts, Interstate Commerce Commission reports, vol. ii, p. 365.

[9] Interstate Commerce Commission reports, vol. ii, p. 365.

[10] Titusville and Oil City Independents' cases. Exhibits, pp. 6, 7, 10.

in August.[11] No attention was paid to this by the road. The Commission waited until October 10th, and then sent a formal communication to the President of the Pennsylvania Railroad, which was followed by correspondence and personal conferences with him. The Commission pointed out that the statement of the circular was "misleading," "not true," "decidedly objectionable"; that the Commission had made no decision with reference to the rates of the Pennsylvania Railroad or the other Eastern lines; that its decision, applicable solely to the roads of the South or Southwest, had been that rates on barrels must be reduced, and that it was not right to use this as an excuse for increasing the rates on barrels. Finally, the Commission said that if it had made any ruling applicable to the Pennsylvania Railroad it would have been compelled to hold that its practice, of twenty years' standing, of carrying the barrels free, since it carried tanks free, was "just and proper," and that there was nothing to show that an advance in its rates was called for.[12]

The Interstate Commerce Commission was the body specially created by Congress to interpret the Interstate Commerce Law. The Pennsylvania Railroad was one of the common carriers under the orders of the Commission, and its managers were subjects of jurisdiction, not judges. But its method of running the Supreme Court of Pennsylvania, as if it were one of its limited trains, was now applied with equal confidence to the Interstate Commerce Commission. It insisted that it was itself, not the Commission, which was the judge of what the latter meant by its own decisions. The road continued the rates against which the Commission protested. The Commission demanded that the assertions that the new rule of charging for the barrels and the advance of rates was made "in accordance with the directions" of the Interstate Commerce Commission be withdrawn. The Pennsylvania road responded with another circular, in which it changed the form but repeated the substance. "The action referred to was taken for the purpose of conforming the practice of this company to the principles decided by the Interstate Commerce Commission." The Commission protested that it was not laying down any such "principles," but the corporation declared that that was what it "understood," and held to the advance made on that understanding.[13]

[11] Interstate Commerce Commission reports, vol. ii., p. 365.
[12] Interstate Commerce Commission reports, vol. ii., p. 365.
[13] Interstate Commerce Commission reports, vol. ii., p. 365.

To the almost weeping expostulations of the Commission in interviews and letters, to show that it had said nothing which could justify the action of the roads, the officials made not the slightest concession. "I did not consider it in that way," said one of them.[14] "That was their (the Commission's) view of the case, but it was not shared by us," said the President of the Pennsylvania Railroad. "It was considered best to continue the practice," he said.[15]

"Why did you not rescind the order?" he was asked before the Interstate Commerce Commission.

"We understood their ruling to be a ruling for the whole country," he incorrigibly replied.

The railway president studiously withheld any assurance that he would obey if the Commission issued a direct command, which it had not done, though it had the authority.

"We would then take the subject up," he said.

Change the order to comply with the ruling of the Interstate Commerce Commission the roads would not and did not.[16]

All the roads to the seaboard and New England had made the order in concert, and together they maintained it. It was one hand, evidently, that moved them all, and though that hand moved them, for the benefit of a carrier rival of theirs—the pipe line of the trust —against their own customers, against their own employers, against the authority of the United States Government, all these railroad presidents and freight agents obeyed it with the docility of domestic animals.

These officials were the loyal subjects of a higher power than that of the United States, higher even than that of their railway corporations. They serve the greatest sovereign of the modern world—the concentrated wealth, in whose court the presidents of railways and republics, kings, parliaments and congresses are but lords in waiting.

Thanks to the superior enterprise of their greater need, the independents of Oil City and Titusville had been able to survive the blows that had preceded, but this was too much. They had weathered the surrender in 1883 of the Tidewater Pipe Line, which had promised them freedom forever. Even the "contract" which made the allied pipe lines and the railroads in 1885 one, to tax them half as much again for transportation, had not broken them down. In spite of it they had been able to "maintain and increase their

---

[14] Testimony, Titusville and Oil City Independents' cases, p. 462.
[15] *Ibid.*, pp. 542, 543.
[16] *Ibid.*, p. 542.

business." [17] But now they closed their works. The new attack had been shrewdly timed to spoil for them in that year—1888—the season of greatest activity in the export to Europe and Asia. They appealed to the Interstate Commerce Commission. "The greater proportion of our refineries are idle." [18] "I have not a customer in the entire New England States. I have not had since the advance of last September."

"How was it before the advance?"

"I had a number of customers." [19]

Two months later most of what remained of the business of the independents in New England was added to the gift of their foreign trade, which had already been made to the "seaboard refiners." By an order of October 25, 1888, the railroads made it known to these "pestilences," as the lawyers of the railroads called the independent refiners in court,[20] that they would not be allowed to send any more through shipments into New England. This was done, as in Ohio in 1879,[21] without the notice required by law, though in the meantime a Federal law had been passed requiring notice.[22]

The independents were saved by a Canadian railroad from the destruction which American railroads had planned for them. The Grand Trunk gave them a rate by which they could still do some business in the upper part of New England, though to do this they had to ship the oil into Canada and back into the United States. The effect of this abolition of through rates in "cheapening" oil was that the people of Vermont, for instance, had to pay 2 cents a gallon more than any other place in New England.[23]

While all access for others to New England was cut off, the "seaboard refiners," sending the oil in free tanks to the seaboard, transshipping it there into vessels by the facilities of "which they have a monopoly," [24] easily made their own the business of their rivals in the 150 towns from which the latter were thus cut off. No one has been able to move all the railroads in this way, as one interlocking switch, to obey a law or accommodate the public. But it was done easily enough for this kind of work. Possession was got of the railway

[17] Titusville and Oil City Independents' cases. Petition and Complaint.
[18] Testimony, Titusville and Oil City Independents' cases, pp. 44, 110, 393, 396.
[19] Ibid., p. 401.
[20] See pp. 69-70.
[21] See ch. xiii.
[22] Testimony, Titusville and Oil City Independents' cases, pp. 283-84.
[23] Ibid., p. 283.
[24] Titusville and Oil City Independents' cases, Interstate Commerce Commission Reports, vol. v., p. 415.

managers at the initial points, as was done so successfully in another case,[25] and all the other railway managers, as far as Boston, followed in their trail. Reproducing the tactics in Ohio in 1879, it was only against oil that this attack of the tariff was made. Other freight for export, of which there was a vast variety, continued to be carried to Boston at the same rate as before.[26]

It would tax the imagination of a Cervantes to dream out a more fantastic tangle of sense and nonsense in quixotic combat than that which these highwaymen spun out of the principles of "scientific railroading." All that highway control could do to destroy the barrel shippers for the benefit of the tank shippers was done; and yet the barrel method is the safer and more profitable for the railroads.[27] The cars that carry oil in barrels can return loaded; the railroads have to haul the tank-cars back empty and pay mileage on them.[28] For a series of years on the Pennsylvania Railroad the damage from carrying oil in barrels was less than half the damage from the carrying of oil in tanks.[29] The general freight agent of the Pennsylvania Railroad Company tells the Interstate Commerce Commission that the carriage of oil in tank-cars "is the most undesirable business we do." He described a smash-up at New Brunswick where there was a collision with a line of tank-cars. The oil got on fire; it ran two squares, got into a sewer, overflowed the canal, which was then frozen over, and followed the ice a square or two beyond. Besides having to pay nearly five hundred thousand dollars damages for the destruction done, the railroad lost its bridge, which cost two or three hundred thousand dollars. It lost more money than it could make carrying oil for ten years. "I regard it," he said, "as worse than powder to carry; I would rather carry anything else than oil in tanks." [30] Barrel shipments being the best for the railroads, these princes of topsy-turvydom move heaven and earth to destroy them.[31]

[25] See chs. xiii, xvi, xvii.
[26] Testimony, Titusville and Oil City Independents' cases, pp. 268-336.
[27] Ibid., p. 296.
[28] Ibid., Testimony of General Freight Manager of the Lehigh Valley Railroad, pp. 161-162.
[29] Ibid., Testimony of General Freight Agent of the Pennsylvania Railroad, pp. 523, 537.
[30] Testimony of General Freight Agent of the Pennsylvania Railroad in Nicolai and Brady vs. Pennsylvania Railroad et al., before Interstate Commerce Commission, Jan. 23, 1888.
[31] The new rates prohibited the traffic. Testimony, Titusville and Oil City Independents' cases, pp. 97, 110, 139, 141, 146-48, 383-84; 393, 396, 397, 400, 401, 402.

There was no end to the "mistakes" made by the railroads for the "self-renunciation" of their business, though this was in favor of those whose pipe line made them rivals. They charged more for kerosene in barrels than for other articles of more value, contradicting their own rule of charging what the traffic will bear. They let the combination carry sixty-two gallons in every tank free on the theory of leakage in transportation. "The practice," said the Commission, "is so obvious and palpable a discrimination that no discussion of it is necessary"; and they ordered it discontinued.[32]

Though the railroads brought back the tanks free, for the return of the empty barrels they never forgot to charge. This charge was made so high that at one time it prohibited the return from all points.[33] "The monopoly uses a large number of barrels in New York City," the independents said to the Commission; "it is to its interest that empty secondhand barrels should not be returned to the inland refiner." When this was brought out the Pennsylvania and other railroads promised to make reparation, but had not done so years later when the case was still "hung up" in the Interstate Commerce Commission.

It was not lack of capital or of diligence that made the independents use barrels instead of tanks; tanks were useless to them. All the oil terminal facilities of the railroads at the seaboard had been surrendered to the combination for its exclusive use.[34] These were the only places where tank-cars could be unloaded into steamers. "There are no facilities to which we, as outside refiners, have access to load bulk oil into vessels," and none where these refiners could send oil in tank-cars to be barrelled for shipment abroad.[35] No matter how many tank-cars and tank-vessels the independents might have provided, they could not have got them together. Between the two were the docks in the unrelenting grip which held solely for its private use the shipping facilities of these public carriers. Not even oil in barrels could the independents get through these oil docks.

Such was the story told to the Interstate Commerce Commission, in many hundred pages of testimony, by the refiners of Oil City and Titusville, who appealed to it for the justice "without expense, without delay, and without litigation" promised the people when the

[32] Decision in Rice, Robinson, and Witherop case, Interstate Commerce Commission Reports, vol. iv., p. 131.
[33] Testimony, Titusville and Oil City Independents' cases, p. 282.
[34] New York Assembly "Hepburn" Report, 1879, p. 44.
[35] Testimony, Titusville and Oil City Independents' cases, p. 36.

Interstate Commerce Commission was created.[36] The game, of which you have perhaps been able to get a dim idea from the printed page, the Commissioners saw played before them like chess with living figures. For years the principal subject of their official investigations had been the manoeuvres of the oil ring. They had been compelled by the law and the facts to condemn its relation with the railroads in language of stinging severity, as every court has done before which it has been brought. Better than any other men in the country, except the men in the ring, the Commissioners knew what was being done. They comprehended perfectly who the "seaboard refiners" were whose demand that their competitors should be shut out of Europe and New England was better law with the Pennsylvania Railroad than the decisions of the Commission. They needed no enlightenment as to the purpose of the secret contract between the members of the oil trust and the Pennsylvania, nor any instruction that the "pool" between the pipe line and the railroad was as hostile to the public interest as any pool between common carriers.

The chairman of the Commission had openly hinted that the relations of the oil trust and the railroads were collusive, and that the spring from which they flowed was a secret contract.[37] It was shown to the Commission that at the same time the railroads advanced their rates the oil combination bid up the price of the raw material of the Titusville and Oil City refineries. This is called "advancing the premium." [38] The raise of the freight rate added 14 cents a barrel to the cost of production, and the increased price of oil put on 12 cents more, either item large enough to embarrass competition. The Interstate Commerce Commission in its decision recognized the practical simultaneity of the three movements to the disadvantage of the independent refiners: (1) the bidding up of the price of crude oil against them; (2) the new rule of charging for the weight of the barrel; and (3) the abrogation of the through rates to New England. These three things occurred in a period of about two months. This, the Commission says, lends color to the charge that there was concert of action between the combination and the railroad.

The defendant corporations, and their lawyers, officers, and witnesses, made no pretence of treating the Interstate Commerce Com-

[36] Report of Senate Select Committee, Interstate Commerce, 49th Congress, 1st Session, 1886, p. 214.
[37] Testimony, Titusville and Oil City Independents' cases, p. 252.
[38] Ibid., pp. 20, 45, 75, 128-29, 175-77.

mission with anything more than a physical respect. The representatives of the railroad companies practically told the Commission that its decisions were subordinate to theirs, and that they knew better than it what its rulings meant. Witnesses refused to answer questions they found awkward, and the lawyers gave the court to understand that if it did what they did not like they would snuff it out. The Commission heard one of the refiners who was a petitioner before it assailed with coarse vituperation, described in open court as a "pestilence," [39] because he had dared to write more than once to the railroads for a reduction of rates which would save him from destruction, and which the Commission had, not once, but half a dozen times, said the railroads ought to give to all.

The Commission had itself, outrunning the complainants, been the first to "pointedly disapprove" the attempt to destroy the barrel shippers, and to call upon the railroads to rescind their action. This protest it had made repeatedly—first with the subalterns, then with the chief of the Pennsylvania Railroad, in personal interviews, letters, and finally in an official pamphlet, which was an appeal to the public to judge between it and the corporation. It had reiterated its protest in a formal decision rendered September 5, 1890, after deliberating seven months on the evidence and arguments. In this "they recalled the fact, now almost ancient history, that" the change was "pointedly disapproved by the Commission" when first made, and with lamentations noted that, though almost two years had passed, "the carriers have failed to comply with the suggestions there made. In charging for the weight of the barrels as well as the oil, the carriers that make use of both modes of transportation have disregarded the principles plainly and emphatically laid down by the Commission in the cases cited, and have paid no attention to the subsequent official memorandum explanatory of the decisions in those cases, but have persisted in maintaining a discrimination against barrel shippers. An order requiring the discontinuance of the discrimination has therefore become necessary." [40]

An order has therefore become necessary. The Commission then ordered one road concerned in this separate case to "cease and desist" within thirty days. Although several cases affecting a number of refiners and a number of roads had been heard and submitted together, as practically one in traffic, territory, circumstances, and the main question, it confined its decision to the case which in-

[39] Testimony, Titusville and Oil City Independents' cases, p. 486.
[40] Interstate Commerce Commission Reports, vol. iv., p. 131.

volved only one road, and that a subordinate. There the Commission stopped; and there it stuck for more than two years, from September 5, 1890, to November 14, 1892, refraining from a decision in the case of the principal offender, the Pennsylvania Railroad.

July 15, 1891, the refiners said to the Commission: "Two and one-half years have elapsed since these complaints were filed, and the end is not yet. We earnestly hoped that we had succeeded in convincing this Commission that this respondent was inflicting on complainants a great and unnecessary wrong, which merited the most speedy remedy and redress possible. If we have failed in this we are unable to ascribe the failure to a lack of evidence or promptness in presenting it. It was not thought possible that all this great length of time would be required to reach a conclusion in these matters, under all these circumstances, especially after the decision in the Rice, Robinson, and Witherop case (September 5, 1890). The enemies of the complainants could scarcely have found or wished for any more effectual way of injuring complainants than by a long delay of their cause. Further delay simply means further injury to complainants." The two years and a half have gone on to more than five years. A decision has been made, but the end is not yet. The delay prevented the injured men from going to any other tribunal with their complaint. They have succeeded in keeping alive, though barely alive, because the price of their raw material has declined a little, and given them a margin to cling to. This delay has denied them justice in the special tribunal they were invited to attend, and has also denied them the relief they could have got from other courts.

The Commission heard all this urged by eloquent counsel. It heard the men who were being crushed tell how their refineries were being closed, their customers lost, their business wrecked, their labor idle, while the trade itself was growing larger than ever. It saw the statistics which proved it. But no practical relief have the independents of Oil City and Titusville been able to get from it. They have lost the business, lost the hopes of five years, lost the growth they would have made, lost five years of life.

This delay of justice is awful, but it is not the end, for the decision, though it came at last in November, 1892, has brought no help. It required the roads to either carry the barrels free or furnish tankcars to all shippers, and for the past ordered a refund of the freight charged on barrels to shippers who had been denied the use of tank-cars. More than five months after it was rendered the independents, in an appeal (April 20, 1893) to the Interstate Commerce Commission, called its attention to the fact that "none of the railroads in any one of the cases has as yet seen fit to obey any of its orders save such and to such extent as they found them advantageous to themselves, although the time for doing so has expired." More appalling still, it appeared, in an application made in March, 1893, by the Pennsylvania Railroad for a re-opening of the case, that these years of litigation were but preliminary to further litigation. The counsel of the railroad, in the spirit in which it had previously warned the Commission that its powers "may be tested," now informed it that the road, if the application for further delay were not granted, would "await proceedings in the Circuit Court for enforcement of what it believed to be an erroneous order." And in another passage it referred to the proceedings before the Commission as being simply proceedings "in advance of any final determination of the case on its merits." Four years and a half had been consumed when, as the independents pleaded to the Commission, "it might reasonably have been expected that as many months would have sufficed," and yet these are only preliminary to "the final determination of the case on its merits."

"The delay suffered has been despairing—killing," was the agonized cry of the independents in their plea to the Interstate Commerce Commission not to grant this new delay. "We pray that no more be permitted." But in November, 1893, more delay was permitted by granting another application of the Pennsylvania Railroad for "rehearing." This was limited to thirty days, but these have run into months, and "the end is not yet." Five years have now passed in this will-o'-the-wisp pursuit of justice "without delay."

The secret contract stands, but the barrel men survive, barely, despite monopoly, by changing to tank-cars, and getting a pipe-line and some terminals. They create seaboard facilities and persuade the Jersey Central to haul their tanks. To meet this road they lay the pipe now to be described, and, to escape railroads altogether, will build to New York, if not ruined meanwhile.

XIII

Purchase of Peace

Hunting about for tax-dodgers, it was discovered by the authorities of Pennsylvania some years ago that many foreign corporations were doing business within the limits of the Commonwealth and enjoying the protection of her laws, and at the same time not paying for it. Foremost among these delinquents stood the principal company in the oil combination with its mammoth capital, practically buying, refining and controlling nearly the entire oil production of the state, "and yet failing to pay one cent into the public treasury." So wrote the Auditor-General to his successor in 1882. The combination, beginning, like creation, with nothing, had grown, until in 1883 it was so rich that, according to the testimony of one of its members, it owned "between $40,000,000 and $50,000,000" in Pennsylvania alone.[1] But though doing business in Pennsylvania, and legally within the grasp of the taxing power, as decided by the courts, this company paid no taxes, and would not give the State the information called for by law as to its taxable property. It practised "voluntary taxation." "For eight years," Auditor-General Schell says, "it had been doing business in this Commonwealth, and had failed in all that time to file a single report." "It was not necessary for the department to call upon it to make reports." The law required these reports specifically and in details that could not be misunderstood, and that was notification enough. But year after year the Auditor-Generals, whose duty it was to collect due contribution from each taxpayer, made special demands upon this one for reports in compliance with the law, but with no effect.

In 1878 William P. Schell became Auditor-General, and began,

[1] Proceedings of Joint Committee Pennsylvania Legislature on Standard Oil Company and its Taxes, 1883, p. 527.

shortly after taking his oath, to see if he could find out what taxes
were due from this concern, and how they could be collected. He
sent official circulars to the company in 1878, 1879, 1880, but "there
was no reply made at any time." [2] His predecessor had had the same
experience. He then sent one of his force to Pittsburg, Philadelphia,
and New York to investigate. Whenever he could get the names of
persons familiar with the workings of the company he would visit
them, to find himself usually "not much further ahead than when he
started." [3] "It was impossible to get any information. Even the men
we talked to deceived us. Men came to Harrisburg to give us information, and afterwards we found they were in the interests of
the company." [4] The department found itself, the Auditor-General
wrote to his successor, "foiled at all points, not only by the refusal
of the company to respond to the notices sent to its officers, but also
by the great reticence of all persons in any manner connected with
or employed by the company."

These efforts to find out the nature and character of the business
of the company extended through two or three years. The first
workable indication that the company was taxable in Pennsylvania
came when the Governor of Ohio, in answer to inquiries, sent the
Attorney-General a copy of the charter of the company. The Auditor-General wrote to the Governor and Auditor-General of New
York and the Governor of Ohio for information. Letters were sent
to the president and principal members of the company at Cleveland, Oil City, New York, and elsewhere. An answer was finally
received from the company's attorney. He said that the company
was not subject to taxation. The department replied the same day
refusing to accept this view, and insisting on reports. Then the
lawyer replied that the books and papers "were at Cleveland, and it
would take some time to prepare reports." The Auditor-General
offered to send his clerk to Cleveland "by first train," to prepare the
reports for the company if assurance was given that he would be
permitted to examine the books of the company when he got there.

No reply to this request was ever received. Then telegrams were
sent, several days in succession, asking for reports, offering more
time if the company would agree to report within any reasonable
time, and finally warning the company that if it did not comply

[2] Proceedings of Joint Committee Pennsylvania Legislature on Standard Oil
Company and its Taxes, 1883. Testimony of Auditor-General Schell, p. 11 et seq.,
pp. 394-95, and of Corporation Clerk, ibid., p. 58, et seq.
[3] Ibid., pp. 60, 61, 62.
[4] Ibid., pp. 374, 383.

with the law and file its reports the Auditor-General would act under the authority given him by the law, and charge it with taxes estimated on such "reasonable data" as he could procure. All the department could get were evasive letters or telegrams from the counsel in New York, such as "letter explaining on the way." The letter came with the valuable information that "the officers are out of the city, and the company will answer on their return." Another "reply" was: "I have failed to get replies from the absent officers." [5] No reports forthcoming, the Auditor-General at last, on the best information he could get, backed by affidavits which were placed on file in the archives of his office, calculated the taxes due from 1872 to 1881, with penalties, at $3,145,541.64. This was totalled on an estimate, supported by affidavit, that the profits of the company had been two to three millions a year from 1872 to 1876, and ten to twelve millions a year from 1876 to 1880, figures which what is now known show to have been near the truth. After fixing upon this amount, and before charging it against the company, the latter was given still another chance, and another. Two telegrams were sent notifying that the estimated tax would be entered up if "the refusal to report" was persisted in. The last telegram said: "Still hoping that reports will come from the company, so that we will have some data to act upon."

No word of reply came.

Then the Auditor-General formally entered the amount he had estimated on his books, as the law authorized him to do.[6] His investigations had consumed his entire term, and the filing of this estimate was almost his last official act. It is a fact of record that after all this, officers of the company, in seeking to have this estimate of taxes due set aside, stated in writing that "there was no neglect or refusal on the part of said company to furnish any report or information which could lawfully be required of it by any officer or under any law of the State of Pennsylvania." [7]

Suit was now brought by the Attorney-General of the State to recover this tax, as was his duty, and then the company began to stir itself. To assist him in procuring and interpreting evidence the Attorney-General, who knew nothing of the oil business, obtained

[5] Proceedings of Joint Committee Pennsylvania Legislature on Standard Oil Company and its Taxes, 1883, pp. 68, 69, 70, 381.

[6] Proceedings of Joint Committee Pennsylvania Legislature on Standard Oil Company and its Taxes, 1883, pp. 53, 70, 81-85.

[7] Appeal of Standard Oil Company to the Court of Common Pleas of Dauphin County, Pennsylvania, June 20, 1881.

the services of a man who knew more about it than any one else in Pennsylvania. This person was a practical oil man. He was one of the leaders of the producers and refiners' association, which in the exciting times of 1872, when law and order in Pennsylvania stood on the edge of a crater, compelled the railroads to abandon the South Improvement scheme, "in name," and to give in writing the pledge that "all arrangements for the transportation of oil after this date shall be upon the basis of perfect equality to all," though he could not find a way to make them keep the pledge.

The members of the great corporation saw that they must act. In out-going Auditor-General Schell they had met the first officer of the people who was as determined to make them pay as they were not to pay. The policy of silence and nullification was abandoned. One of the members of the trust came in person to the State capital to see the Attorney-General. He made an unexpected overture. He volunteered to furnish the State with a full disclosure of the facts it needed to prove its claim.

"I confess," said the Deputy Attorney-General, "that I little knew in what direction to cross-examine him." [8] He therefore sent for the expert who had been employed by the Attorney-General. The "trustee" protested against his presence; but the Deputy Attorney-General said that he had been employed by the State, and it would be necessary that he should take part. The representative of the trust, moved, as he afterwards testified, by the patriotic consideration that "the regular cumbersome way of taking oral testimony . . . would result in great labor and expense to the State, and would be an obstruction and labor to us that could be avoided," made a suggestion that the State go to the trial of the case upon a statement of facts of their business which he and his associates would make. This offer to become a volunteer witness was agreed to, and the delinquent corporation and the State went into court with an "agreement as to facts." The Attorney-General reserved for the State the right to add to these facts, but did not at any time during the proceedings do so.

From the Attorney-General, who knew little of either the facts, as he confessed, or the law as the court declared it, who accepted their statements as gospel, and who asked them whether new facts offered him should be admitted into his side of the case against them, the company had nothing to fear. But this old opponent of

[8] Proceedings of the Joint Committee of the Pennsylvania Legislature, etc., pp. 143, 196, 476.

theirs, whom the Attorney-General had employed, was at large, and was a dangerous man. He knew the facts; he had the right theory of the law; he was tremendously in earnest. The case had only got as far as the first decision of the lower court. There were still opportunities for all kinds of legal proceedings. By virtue of this contract he claimed such an interest in the proceedings as to give him a right to ask the courts to interfere. He might get a new trial and carry out his "pet scheme of oral examination." He might rouse the people as he had roused them before. He might interfere through the Legislature. He might raise a storm which could not be quieted until in this suit, or some other, his pet plan might be carried out, of getting these silent gentlemen into a witness-box. He considered himself to be in the service of the State. "I was under a contract with the State," [9] he says. And we find the Attorney-General in close consultation with him in Philadelphia down to the very last day.

The company sees that something must be done, and does it. Its "trustee" calls upon the expert at his hotel.[10] He renews the suggestion he had made in New York when word had been sent by the expert that he would not be bound by the agreement of facts, and "proposed to attack." He finds his man cast down, utterly discouraged by the decision of the lower court and the attitude of the Attorney-General. Time and again he had seen the people denied justice, and their enemies escape even so much as the necessity of appearing in court. He had seen, in every one of the proceedings against them, from 1872 to 1880, committees of Congress, State governors, judges of the Supreme courts, State legislatures, attorney-generals, railroad officials, every trustee of the people, wilt, like green leaves in a fire, before this flashing wealth. His resolution gave way. He was to have received, under his agreement with the Attorney-General, in salary and commissions, $23,000, or less, according to the amount recovered. That he saw fading out of sight in consequence of the, to him, inexplicable course of the Attorney-General. Every one else who had tried to stand up for the people against this power had gone down; why should he be quixotic and poor?

"We want peace," the "trustee" said, and the, till then, faithful friend of the people sold him all he had of that commodity for $15,400, to be paid in instalments, and a salary of $5000 for a year.

[9] Proceedings of the Joint Committee of the Pennsylvania Legislature, etc., pp. 640-43, 830.
[10] *Ibid.*, p. 231.

"I proposed to reopen it"—the case—"and I did not."

"Why did you not?"

"Simply because I was assured I should have just as much money out of the transaction, as my original contract would have paid me."

This confession made on the stand, under the strain of cross-examination in a civil suit in which he was a witness, startled the country with its first hint of the real cause of the failure of the great tax case, and led to an investigation by the Legislature of Pennsylvania.[11]

The committee of the Legislature appointed to investigate this "purchase of peace" furnishes in its report the facts we have recited, which were uncontradicted, but declares that the transactions they disclose "did not prejudice the rights of the Commonwealth," and that nobody had done anything wrong. An effort was made after the failure of the tax case to get the Attorney-General of the State to issue a warrant against the purchaser of peace, upon which he could have been held to trial in a criminal court for bribery and corrupt solicitation of a public officer. An affidavit charging the crime in the usual form was presented to the Attorney-General. There was by this time a new Attorney-General, but he ditched this move with the same skill for the management of his adversaries' case that his predecessor had exhibited in the tax suit. He demanded that affidavit be made by some one who could testify to the bribery of his personal knowledge before the committing magistrate. As the facts were known only to the two principals, and neither of them could be expected to come forward to make affidavit and application for his own commitment, the Attorney-General demanded the impossible.[12] The fact of bribery was publicly known by the confession under oath of one of these principals, and the Attorney-General had been presented with the affidavit of a citizen, prepared in due and regular form, upon which he could have proceeded to issue a warrant, as is done in the case of less powerful offenders. Failing with the Attorney-General to have this transaction taken into the courts, the effort was renewed with the committee the Legislature had appointed to investigate. It was asked to do as committees had done before—to send the case to a criminal court and let it be tried. The distinguished lawyer acting for the people before

[11] Proceedings of the Joint Committee of the Pennsylvania Legislature, etc., pp. 229-30, 284-95.

[12] Proceedings of the Joint Committee of the Pennsylvania Legislature, etc., p. 661.

the committee offered to appear as a volunteer Attorney-General in the prosecution of the trustee. "There is not an honest jury," he said, "in the state of Pennsylvania which upon the testimony would not send him to the penitentiary for the crime of bribery." [13] The committee refused to send the matter to the courts.

Upon the only occasion when the "Trustees" seemed in real danger of being brought in person and on specific charges to trial, criminally, the Supreme Court of Pennsylvania saved them. In the Clarion County cases it took the unprecedented step of interfering with the criminal jurisdiction of the lower courts. It was in reference to this that Mr. Gowen said before the Committee of Commerce of Congress in 1880: "I was a member of the Constitutional Convention of Pennsylvania, and I know that if that convention did anything effectively it was when it declared that the Supreme Court should not have original jurisdiction in criminal cases, and yet I have seen three judges of the Supreme Court lay their hands upon an indictment in a county court and hang it up." The effect of this interposition of the Supreme Court is summed up as follows in the history of the contest between the Producers' Union and their powerful antagonists: "This practically terminated the last legal proceeding conducted by the general council of the producers of petroleum." "It was the greatest violation of law," said Mr. Gowen before the Pennsylvania Legislative Committee, "ever committed in the Commonwealth." [14]

That some such action might have been expected could be inferred from the remark in *Leading Cases Simplified*, by John D. Lawson, warning the student of the law of carriers "not to pay much heed to the decisions of the Supreme Court of Pennsylvania —at least, during the past ten or fifteen years. The Pennsylvania Railroad appears to run that tribunal with the same success that it does its own trains." [15]

Some time after these events the purchaser of this peace gave some money to a hospital for cancers, and, in recognition of his philanthropy, was made its president. This hospital was for cancers of the body—not for moral cancers of the kind propagated for money by men who corrupt the Commonwealth. It would have been full expiation in the good old times of the priest and the baron Ruskin

[13] *Ibid.*, F. B. Gowen, p. 650.
[14] Proceedings of the Joint Committee of the Pennsylvania Legislature, etc., p. 713.
[15] Hudson's *Railways and Republic*, p. 465.

describes to donate to the cure of an evil a fraction of the profits of
the culture of it. The newspapers in May, 1891, chronicled the
opening of another pavilion of this hospital, and the delivery of "an
interesting address" by the new president. One of the journals
remarks that "this interest, combined with his well-known liberality
in Church and humane matters generally, suggests a thought concerning the peculiar development on this line of many of our very
rich men." But what the "thought" was the journalist did not go on
to state.

XIV

"I Want to Make Oil"

"The first successful pipe line," says the United States Census
Report of 1885, "was put down by Samuel Van Syckel, of Titusville,
in 1865, and extended from Pithole to Miller's Farm, a distance of
four miles." [1]

"I hit on the pipe-line idea," said Van Syckel, "and announced
that I would carry the oil by pipe from the wells to the railroad.
That was too much for the people of the oil regions. Everybody
laughed me down. Even my particular friends, with whom I used to
take my meals at the hotel, jeered and gibed me so that I took to
coming and going through the back door and through the kitchen,
and ate by myself. 'Do you expect to put a girdle around the
earth?' was the favorite sarcasm. I knew it would cost a great deal
—$100,000 perhaps; but I had the money. I built it—two two-inch
lines, side by side—between June and November in 1865, and
turned the oil in. The pipe was a perfect success from the first
barrel of oil that was pumped in. It flowed, just as I expected, up
hill and down dale. The line was four miles long—from the Miller
Farm to Pithole—with two or three branches.[2]

The rest of the old man's story was told by him under oath in a
suit he brought against members of the combination.[17] "The idea of
continuous distillation, as it was suggested to me at Jersey City, was
always in my brain ever since. I made an attempt to construct such
works in 1876 under Mr. Cary. I run out of money. I had been
robbed out of my pipe line that cost me $100,000, and my oil-

---

[1] "Petroleum and Its Products," by S. F. Peckham, Special Agent, U.S. Census,
1885, p. 93.
[2] Samuel Van Syckel vs. Acme Oil Company. Tried in the Supreme Court at
Buffalo, N.Y., May 14, 1888.

refinery in which I had more than $100,000. Mr. Cary said he was
going to build a little refinery. He said he had $10,000 that we
might use in making oil in a continuous way. We got our lease and
broke ground in 1876. We had not got very far—we got the pipe on
the ground and some brick and one old-fashioned still—when" the
representative of the oil combination, one of its principal members,
"came on to the ground . . . the 15th of December, 1876. He asked
me if I would not take a salary and not build these works in opposition to them. I told him 'No.' Then he wanted I should take a
life salary, one that would support me for life comfortably. I told
him I did not want his salary; I wanted to build this refinery and
make oil in a new continuous way. He then wanted me to let him
build it. He said, 'We will build it for you.' I objected to this. He
then said that I could make no money if I did refine oil. He also
said if I did I could not ship it. He said he would say to me confi-
dentially that they had made such arrangements with the railroads
in reference to freight—in reference to getting cars—he knew I
could make no money if I did make oil."

Almost on the same day—May 14, 1888—on which Van Syckel
was giving the jury this undisputed account, sustained by the judge
and jury, of how the combination used "arrangements with the
railroads" against its rivals, another pioneer, even more distinguished, was relating his almost identical experience before the
committee of Congress investigating trusts, May 3, 1888. This was
Joshua Merrill, "to whom," said S. Dana Hayes, State Chemist of
Massachusetts, "more than to any one else, belongs the honor of
bringing this manufacture to its present advanced state." [3] Merrill's
inventions and successful labors are described in the United States
Census Report on Petroleum, 1885. He was at work guessing the
riddles of petroleum as long ago as 1854.[4]

From 1866 to 1888 he and his partners ran a refinery at Boston.
"What has become of it?"
"We have recently dismantled it." [5]

For several years their business had been unprofitable. There
were two causes, he explained. One was that they made a better
quality of oil than the average, at a cost which they could not
recoup from the prices established in the market by poorer oils.

[3] *The Early and Later History of Petroleum*, by J. G. Henry, 1873, p. 186.
[4] "Petroleum and Its Products," by S. F. Peckham, Special Agent, U.S. Census,
1885, p. 9.
[5] Trusts, Congress, 1888, Testimony of Joshua Merrill, p. 566.

The other cause was the extraordinary charges made against his firm by the railways in Boston which brought their crude.

His firm had their own tank-cars, in which their crude oil came from Pennsylvania. From Olean to Boston his freight cost him the last few years 50 cents a barrel. From the depot in Boston, to get it over two miles of track to his refinery, cost him $10 a car, or about $1.25 a barrel. This was at the rate of about 42½ cents a ton a mile. The average freight rate for the United States is about half a cent a ton a mile. His rate was an advance of 8400 per cent. on the average. He appealed to the Railroad Commission of Massachusetts.

"We wrote to the commissioners that we thought the charge was very high, and they ought to interfere to have it reduced. But it was not done.

"We made repeated efforts, personal solicitations, to the railroad officers, and to the railroad commissioners also, but it was the established rate." [6]

Two roads participated in this charge of $10 for hauling a car two miles. One of these was the New York and New England road, whose haul was a mile and a half, and its charge $6.

"Who was president of the New York and New England road?" The dismantled witness's experience had made him timid.

"I do not know."

"Do you not know," he was asked, "that one of the oil trustees is president?"

"Yes, sir." [7]

The same railroad is the principal New England link in the lines of circumvallation which the combination in coal, hard and soft, American and Nova Scotian, is drawing about the homes and industries of the country. His company sold their tank-cars to the oil combination, as "we no longer had any use for them." [8]

"I was thirty-two years in the oil business," the veteran said, mournfully, as he left the stand. "It was the business of my life." [9]

To return to Van Syckel. After his warning to the inventor that he could get no cars and make no money, even if his new idea proved a success, the representative of the combination invited Van Syckel to put himself in its hands.

"He said they would furnish the money to test the invention and

6 Trusts, Congress, 1888, Testimony of Joshua Merrill, pp. 567-69.
7 Ibid., p. 568.
8 Ibid., p. 568.
9 Ibid., p. 570.

pay me all it was worth. I felt a little startled at the rebates, and I
knew it before, but I did not know it was so bad as he had figured it
out. I then asked him who of his company would agree to furnish
me money to test the patent and to pay all it was worth. He asked
me who I wanted to agree with. I then asked him if a man"
(naming him) "that I had had more or less dealings with" (one of
the trustees) "would agree to what he had said. He said he had no
doubt he would. He said, 'We will go and see him, and go at his
expense.' He said he would take the works off my hands at cost, and
would satisfy my partner to stop building them if I would go to
New York, and I think it was the next day when we went to New
York."

They went to the office of the member of the combination whom
Van Syckel had said he would confide in. "He seemed to be very
glad to see me, and very sorry to learn I had been so unfortunate in
the oil regions. He then asked me what these patent works would
cost in a small way to prove that oil could be successfully made
under continuous distillation. I told him it could be done for about
$10,000. He said they would give it, . . . and if it proved a success
they would give me $100,000. He said it was worth more. He would
give me $125 a month to support my family during the time I was
building and testing it. I said, 'Let us put what we have agreed
upon in writing.' He begged off for a time. He said it could be done
at Titusville just as well. He saw I was not quite satisfied being
cut off in that way, so he took my hand and said he would give me
his word and honor what they had agreed upon there should be
put in writing at Titusville Monday morning. I did not want to
press him any harder. I told him I would take the $125 a month
until the thing was tested. If it proved a failure the whole thing
should come back where it started from, and if it proved a success
he was to pay me $100,000" (for the patents and the business). "He
said we all understood it, then. I went home." Van Syckel called
upon the Titusville member of the trust. "He begged off from me
the same as the other did in New York; said they were pressed with
business. He said they would fix it this afternoon, or words to
that effect." Instead of building for him, as it had agreed, the
combination, the moment he placed himself in its hands, destroyed
the building he had already begun.

When twelve years had gone by, and he found that they would
neither build for him as agreed nor let any one else build for him,

Van Syckel turned to the law and sued them for damages. On the trial all the facts as we have stated were admitted—the abandonment of the enterprise in consequence of the threats that he would not be allowed to ship and market his oil; the interviews in New York; the contract; the sale; Van Syckel's later efforts to make oil in other refineries; his success in producing better and cheaper oil; its popularity; the purchase and destruction of the works using the new method. Not a word of evidence was adduced in disproof. The judge and the jury found all these questions in Van Syckel's favor.

The defence was twofold. It was admitted that the two representatives Van Syckel had dealt with had made the contract as he described it. The members of the combination did not deny that. But, they argued, it was not legally binding. "We simply concede," said these great men to the Court, "that they made a contract, but leaving it to the corporation itself to decide upon it. . . . There cannot be the slightest claim that the company was bound by a contract of that character." On this point they were defeated in the trial. Their second defence was that there were no damages. "The trouble is," they said, "that there are no damages sustained, no damages whatever sustained." They took the ground that his possessing a creative mind was the cause of Van Syckel's ruin, not their betrayal of him. "Mr. Van Syckel," they argued to the Court, sympathetically, "is an instance of what it means to get out a patent, and deal in patents—in nine cases out of ten. He was an inventive man. He has got out a good many patents. No question they were meritorious patents. And what is the result? Poverty, a broken heart, an enfeebled intellect, and a struggle now for the means of subsistence by this lawsuit. So that, if your honor please, there is nothing here from which we can determine what the original value of this patent was." The jury and the judge decided against them, and held there was a contract, legal and binding. That brought them face to face with the question of damages, and here the ruling of the judge saved them, as the decision of another judge saved other members of the combination in the criminal case in the same city, about the same time. The judge ordered the jury to find the damages at six cents, and the jury—in the evolution of freedom juries appear to have become merely clerks of the Court—did so. "This direction of a verdict," said the Court to Van Syckel, "decides every other question of the case in your favor."

Six cents damages for breach of such a contract, and in Buffalo

$250 fine for conspiracy to blow up a rival refinery! Here are figures with which to begin a judicial price-list of the cost of immunity for crimes and wrongs.

Lawyer Moot, Van Syckel's counsel, deferentially asked the Court to suggest where was the defect in the proof of damages. It would be "the wildest speculation and guesswork," the Court said, for the jury to attempt to compute the damages.

"Then the Court is unable to suggest any particular defect in the proof?"

The Court evaded the point of the counsel, and repeated in general terms that there was no testimony upon which a jury could assess damages.

Those whom he was suing did not disprove that, by threats of making it impossible for him to get transportation, they had driven Van Syckel to abandon his own business, and make a contract with them by which they were to pay him $100,000 for his new process, if successful. The Court held the contract binding. They had not furnished the money and works to test the inventions as they had agreed to do; but he had nevertheless gone on and completed the invention, so that patents were granted for it by the government. He had tested the invention in other works, they failing him, and had proved it a success; they had thereupon purchased and destroyed these works; he was beggared, and nobody else under these circumstances could be induced to venture money on his invention. Upon these facts, judicially ascertained, the judge refused to let the jury compute the damages, and ordered them to find the damages "nominal," as another judge sentenced their associates in Buffalo to "nominal" punishment.

"There are many things known to the law," said Parnell to the president of the Special Commission trying the Irish members of Parliament, "which are strange to a non-legal mind."

XV

Sympathetical Cooperation

George Rice, coming from the Green Mountains of Vermont, entered the oil business twenty-nine years ago, when he and it were young. He was one of the first comers. Beginning as a producer in the Pithole region, in the days of its evanescent glory, in 1865, he prospered. Escaping the ruin which overtook those who stayed too long in that too quick sand, he was one of the first to develop the new field at Macksburg, Ohio, and to see the advantages of Marietta, on the Ohio River, as a point for refining. Crude Oil could easily be brought from Ohio and Pennsylvania by barge down the Ohio River. The field he entered was unoccupied. He drove no one out, but built a new industry in a new place. In 1876 he had risen to the dignity of manufacturer, and had a refinery of a capacity of 500 barrels a week, and later of 2000 barrels.

Several other refiners, seeing the advantages of Marietta, had settled there. They who elected themselves to be trustees of the light of the world, thus having the advantages of the place pointed out to them by practical men, determined that Marietta must be theirs. They bought up some of the refiners. Then they stopped buying. Their representative there, afterwards a member of the trust, "told me distinctly that he had bought certain refineries in Marietta, but that he would not buy any more. . . . He had another way," he said, "of getting rid of them." [1] Of these "other ways" the independents were now to have a full exposition. In January, 1879, freight rates on oil were suddenly and without previous notice raised by the railroads leading out of Marietta, and by their connections. Some of the rates were doubled. The increase was only on

[1] Railroad Freights, Ohio House of Representatives, 1879, p. 28.

oil. It was—in Ohio—only on oil shipped from Marietta; it was exacted only from the few refiners who had not been bought, because there were "other ways of getting rid of them." [2]

This freight-tariff attack on the independent refiners was arranged by their powerful rival and the railroad managers at a secret conference, as the latter admitted.

"Did you have any consultation or invite consultation with other manufacturers of oil at Marietta?"

"No, sir." [3]

When the representatives of the combination in this market were taxed by a dealer with getting the benefit of this manipulation of freight, "they laughed." All the railroads took part in the surprise. Curiously enough, the minds of the managers of a dozen roads acted simultaneously and identically, over thousands of miles of country —some, as they admitted, with suggestion, and some, as they testified, without suggestion—upon so precise a detail of their business as the rates on oil at one little point. "I did it at my own instance," said the freight agent of the Baltimore and Ohio. Freight officials of railways as far apart east, west, and south, and in interest, as the Baltimore and Ohio, and the Pennsylvania, and the Lake Shore, which had no direct connection with Marietta, and reached it only over other lines, stopped their "wars" to play their part in the move by raising the rate on oil only, and, most remarkable of all, to a figure at which neither they, nor the railroad connecting them with Marietta, nor (and this was the game they were gunning for) the independent refiners could do any business. From other points than Marietta, as Cleveland, Parkersburg, Pittsburg, and Wheeling, where the combination had refineries, but the Marietta independents had none, the railroads left the former rates unchanged. [4]

Rice was "got rid of" at Columbus just as effectually as if Ruskin's "Money-bag Baron," successor of "the Crag Baron," stood across the road with a blunderbuss. His successful rival had but to let its Marietta refineries lie idle, and transfer to its refineries at Wheeling its Marietta business—and Rice's too. By the pooling of the earnings and of the control of all its refineries—the essential features of the combination—its business could be transferred from one point to another without loss. One locality or another could be subjected to ruinous conditions for the extermination of competi-

[2] Testimony, *ibid.*, pp. 5, 41, 42, 124, 141, 162, 166, 170.
[3] Testimony, *ibid.*, p. 129.
[4] Railroad Freights, Ohio House of Representatives, 1879, pp. 12, 34, 172.

tors, and the combination, no matter how large its works there, would prosper without check. It gets the same profit as before, but the competitor by its side is ruined. All its refineries along a given railroad can be closed by high rates made to "overcome competition," but profits do not cease. Their business is done elsewhere by its other refineries, and all the profits go into a pool for the common benefit.

From Rice's point of view, Marietta was the storm-centre; but the evidence before the Ohio Legislative Investigation of 1879, before the Legislative Committee of New York of 1879, before Master in Chancery Sweitzer in Pennsylvania, and in the suit against the Lake Shore Railroad, showed that the low barometer there was part of a disturbance covering a wide area. The demonstration against the independent refiners of Marietta was only part of a wider web-spinning, in which those at all points—New York, Boston, Philadelphia, Pittsburg, Oil City, Titusville, Buffalo, Rochester, and Cleveland—were to be forced to "come in" as dependents, or sell out, as most of them did.

That rates were not raised from points controlled by the combination is only part of the truth. At such places rates were lowered. This, like the increase of rates, was done at a secret conference with the oil combination and at its instance.[5] Where it had refineries the rates were to be low; the high rates were for points where it had competitors to be got rid of without the expense of buying them up. The independents knew nothing of the increase of freights prepared for them by the railroad managers and their great competitor until after, some time after, it had gone into effect.

The railroad company gave notice to their rivals what the rates were to be, but withheld that information from them.[6] That was not all. Before the new rates were given all the old rates were cancelled. "For a few days," said an independent, "we could not obtain any rates at all. We had orders from our customers, but could not obtain any rates of freight."

As to many places, the withholding of rates continued. "There's many places we can't obtain any rates to. They just say we sha'n't ship to these other places at any price." [7]

When the Ohio Legislature undertook to investigate, it found that the railroad men professed a higher allegiance to their corpora-

[5] Railroad Freights, Ohio House of Representatives, 1879, p. 129.
[6] Trusts, Congress, 1888, p. 579.
[7] Railroad Freights, Ohio House of Representatives, 1879, pp. 33, 40-42.

tions than to the State. They refused to answer the questions of the committee, or evaded them. "I am working under orders from the general freight agent," said one of them, "and I don't feel authorized to answer that." The arguments of the committee that the ord. 's of an employer could not supersede the duty of a citizen to his government, or the obligations of his oath as a witness, were wasted. "I will tell you just how I feel," said the witness to these representatives of an inferior power. "I am connected with the railroad company, and get my instructions from the general agent, and I am very careful about telling anybody else anything." The Legislature accepted the rank of "anybody else" to which it was assigned, and did not compel the witness to answer.

When their "secretary" was called before the Ohio Legislature, after this freight ambuscade had transferred the bulk of the business of the independent refineries at Marietta to him and his associates, he declared that the sole cause of their success was the "large mechanical contrivances" of the combination, its "economy," and its production of the "very best oil." "With an aggregation of capital, and a business experience, and a hold upon the channels of trade such as we have, it is idle to say that the small manufacturer can compete with us; and although that is an offensive term, 'squeezing out,' yet it has never been done by the conjunction of any railroads with us." [8]

The small manufacturer did compete and flourish until these railroad men literally switched him out of the market. He competed and got his share of the business, until the men who wanted monopoly, finding that they had no monopoly of quality or price or business ability, resorted to the "large mechanical contrivance" of inducing the managers of the railroads to derail the independent, throwing him off the track by piling impassable freight tariffs in his way. The successful men secured their supremacy by preventing their competitors from entering the market at all. Instead of winning by "better" and "cheaper," they won by preventing any competitor from coming forward to test the questions of "better" and "cheaper." Their method of demonstrating superiority has been to prevent comparisons.

All the independent refiners at Marietta, except Rice, died. "Most of those we received from have gone out of the business," a Cincinnati dealer told the Legislature. Some had fled; some had

[8] *Ibid.*, p. 260.

sold out.[9] Rice set himself to do two things: the first, to drag into the light of day and the public view the secrets of these "better methods"; and the second, to get new business in the place of what he had lost. He succeeded in both. It was in January that he had notice served upon him that he could no longer go to market. In two months he had the Ohio Legislature at work investigating this extraordinary administration of the highways. This was a great public service. It did not yield the fruit of immediate reform, but it did work which is the indispensable preliminary. It roused the people who were still asleep on these new issues, and were dreaming pleasant dreams that in George III. they had escaped from all tyrants forever, and that in the emancipation of the blacks they had freed all slaves forever.

Rice knew that the Legislature were planting trees for posterity, and did not wait for help from them. He set about looking up markets where the public were free to choose and buy. He could not go West or East or North. He went South. The little family kept the refinery at Marietta running, and the father travelled about establishing new agencies in the South, and studying freight tariffs, railroad routes, and terminal facilities for loading and unloading and storing. In 1880, through all the storm and stress of these days, he was able to double the capacity of his refinery. Again he succeeded in building up a livelihood, and again his success was treated as trespass and invasion. His bitter experience in Ohio in 1879 proved to be but an apprenticeship for a still sterner struggle. Rice was getting most of his crude oil from Pennsylvania, through a little pipe line which brought it to the Alleghany. The pipe line was taken up by the oil trust.[10]

This compelled him to turn to the Macksburg, Ohio, field for most of his petroleum. He had one tank-car, and he ran this back and forth faster than ever. Then came the next blow. The railroad over which he ran his tank-car doubled his freight to 35 cents a barrel, from 17½. That was not all. The same railroad brought oil to the combination's Marietta refineries at 10 cents a barrel, while they charged him 35. That was not all. The railroad paid over to the combination 25 cents out of every 35 cents he paid for freight. If he had done all the oil business at Marietta, and his rival had put out all its fires and let its works stand empty, it would still have made 25 cents a barrel on the whole output. Rice found a just

[9] Railroad Freights, Ohio House of Representatives, 1879, p. 116.
[10] Trusts, Congress, 1888, p. 574.

judge when he took this thing into court. "Abhorrent," "dangerous," "gross," "illegal and inexcusable abuse by a public trust,"
"an unparalleled wrong," are the terms in which Judge Baxter gave
voice to his indignation as he ordered the removal of the receiver
of the railroad who had made this arrangement with the combination, to enable it, as the judge said, "to crush Rice and his
business." [11]

In an interview, filling four columns of the New York *World*
of March 29, 1890, the head of the trust which would receive this
rebate is reported to have made this attempt to reverse the facts
of this and similar occurrences: "The railroad company proposed
to our agent," he said. But the judge who heard all the evidence
and rendered the decision, which has never been reversed or im-
paired, declared that it "compelled" the railroad to make the arrangement, "under a threat of building a pipe line for the con-
veyance of its oils and withdrawing its patronage." This arrangement was negotiated by the same agent of the oil combination who
engineered the similar "transfer" scheme by which the trunk-line
railroads gave it, in 1878, 20 to 35 cents a barrel out of the freights
paid by its competitors in Pennsylvania, as already told.[12]

This "agreement for the transportation of oil" had its calculated
effect. It put a stop to the transportation of oil from the Ohio
field by Rice over the railroad, just as the destruction by the same
hands of the pipe line to the Alleghany had cut him off from access
to the Pennsylvania oil-fields. He then built his own pipe line to
the Ohio field. To lay this pipe it was necessary to cross the pipe
line of his great rival. Rice had the pluck to do this without asking for a consent which would never have been given. His in-
trepidity carried its point, for, as he foresaw, they dared not cut
his pipe for fear of reprisals.

In turning to the South, after his expulsion from the Ohio and
Western markets, the Marietta independent did but get out of one
hornet's nest to sit down in another. His opponent was selling its
oil there through a representative who, as he afterwards told Congress, "was very fortunate in competing." He thought it was
"cheaper in the long-run to make the price cheap and be done with
it, than to fritter away the time with a competitor in a little
competition. I put the price down to the bone." [13] Rice, in the

[11] *Ibid.*, pp. 577-78.
[12] See ch. viii.
[13] Trusts, Congress, 1888, pp. 534, 535.

South, ran into the embrace of this gentleman who had the "exclusive control" of that territory, and whose method of calling the attention of trespassers to his right was to cut them "to the bone." The people and the dealers everywhere in the South were glad to see Rice. He found a deep discontent among consumers and merchants alike. They perhaps felt more clearly than they knew that business feudalism was not better, but worse, because newer, than military feudalism. This representative of the combination assured Congress that "99.9 of all the first-class merchants of the South were in close sympathetical co-operation with us in our whole history"—that is, out of every hundred "first-class merchants" only one-tenth of one merchant was not with them. This is a picturesque percentage.

Rice's welcome among the people would not verify his opponent's estimate that his vassalage included all but one-tenth of one dealer in every hundred. From all parts came word of the anxiety of the merchants to escape from the power that held them fast. From Texas: "Most of our people are anxious to get clear." From Arkansas: "The merchants here would like to buy from some other." From Tennessee: "Can we make any permanent arrangement with you by which we can baffle such monopoly?" From Kentucky: "I dislike to submit to the unreasonable and arbitrary commands." From Mississippi: "It has gouged the people to such an extent that we wish to break it down and introduce some other oils." From Georgia, from different dealers: "They have the oil-dealers in this State so completely cooped in that they cannot move." "We are afraid." [14] As Rice went about the South selling oil the agents of the cutter "to the bone" would follow, and by threats, like those revealed in the correspondence described below, would coerce the dealers to repudiate their purchases. Telegrams would pour into the discouraged office at Marietta: "Don't ship oil ordered from your agent." "We hereby countermand orders given your agent yesterday." One telegram would often be signed by all the dealers in a town, though competitors, sometimes nearly a dozen of them, showing that they were united by some outside influence they had to obey.[15]

Where the dealers were found too independent to accept dictation, belligerent and tactical cuts in price were proclaimed, not to make oil cheap, but to prevent its becoming permanently cheaper

[14] Trusts, Congress, 1888, pp. 730-38.
[15] Trusts, Congress, 1888, p. 743.

through free competition and an open market. Rice submitted to Congress letters covering pages of the Trust Report,[16] showing how he had been tracked through Tennessee, Missouri, Nebraska, Georgia, Kansas, Kentucky, Iowa, Mississippi, Louisiana, Texas, Arkansas, Alabama. The railroads had been got to side-track and delay his cars, and the dealers terrorized into refusing to buy his oils, although they were cheaper. If the merchants in any place persisted in buying his oil they were undersold until they surrendered. When Rice was driven out prices were put back. So close was the watch kept of the battle by the generals of "co-operation" that when one of his agents got out of oil for a day or two, prices would be run up to bleed the public during the temporary opportunity. "On the strength of my not having any oil to-day," wrote one of Rice's dealers, "I am told they have popped up the price 3½ cents." [17]

The railroad officials did their best to make it true that "the poor ye have with you always." By mistake some oil meant for the combination was delivered to Rice's agent, and he discovered that it was paying only 88 cents a barrel, while he was charged $1.68, a difference of 80 cents a barrel for a distance of sixty-eight miles.

"Could you stand such competition as that?"

"No, sir. Before that I went up there and sold to every man in the place nearly. They were glad to see me in opposition. . . . I lost them, except one man who was so prejudiced that he would not buy from them."

"Your business had been on the increase up to that time?"

"Increasing rapidly . . . I haul it in wagons now forty miles south of Manito."

"The rates against you on that railroad are so high that you can for a distance of forty miles transport your oil by wagon and meet the competition better than you can by using their own road?"

"Infinitely better." [18]

[16] *Ibid.*, p. 729.
[17] *Ibid.*, p. 732.
[18] Trusts, Congress, 1888, pp. 416-20.

XVI

"Turn Another Screw"

Rice throughout the South was put under a surveillance which could hardly have been done better by Vidocq.[1] One of the employés of the oil clique, having disclosed before the Interstate Commerce Commission that he knew to a barrel just how much Rice had shipped down the river to Memphis, was asked where he got the information. He got it from the agents who "attend to our business."

"What have they to do with looking after Mr. Rice's business? . . . How do your agents tell the number of barrels he shipped in April, May, and June?"

"See it arrive at the depot."

"How often do your agents go to the depot to make the examination?"

"They visit the depot once a day, not only for that purpose, but to look after the shipment of our own oil."

"Do they keep a record of Mr. Rice's shipments?"

"They send us word whenever they find that Mr. Rice has shipped a car-load of oil."

"What do their statements show with respect to Mr. Rice's shipments besides that?"

"They show the number of barrels received at any point shipped by Mr. Rice, or by anybody else."

"How often are these statements sent to the company?"

"Sent in monthly, I think."

"It is from a similar monthly report that you get the statement

[1] Vidocq: Eugène François Vidocq (1775-1857) was a fabled French detective and secret agent whose service as head of the French detective force was ended when Vidocq was discovered to have committed several of the crimes his staff had under investigation. [T.C.]

that in July, August, and September, Mr. Rice shipped 602 barrels of oil to Nashville, is it?"

"Yes, sir."

"Have you similar agents at all points of destination?"

"Yes, sir." [2]

This has a familiar look. It is the espionage of the South Improvement Company contract, in operation sixteen years after it was "buried." When the representative of the oil combination appears in public with tabulated statements exhibiting to a barrel the business done by its competitors for any month of any year, at any place, he tells us too plainly to be mistaken that the "partly-born," completely "buried" iniquity, sired by the "sympathetical co-operation" of the trustees and their railroad associates of easy virtue, is alive and kicking—kicking a breach in the very foundations of the republic.

A letter has found the light which was sent by the Louisville man who was so "fortunate in competing," immediately after he heard that one of "his" Nashville customers had received a shipment from the Marietta independent. It was addressed to the general freight agent of the Louisville and Nashville Railroad. It complained that this shipment, of which the writer knew the exact date, quantity, destination, and charges, "slipped through on the usual fifth-class rate." "Please turn another screw," the model merchant concluded. What it meant "to turn another screw" became quickly manifest. Not daring to give the true explanation, none of the people implicated have ever been able to make a plausible explanation of the meaning of this letter. The railroad man to whom it was sent interpreted it when examined by Congress as meaning that he should equalize rates. But Congress asked him:

"Is the commercial phrase for equalizing rates among railroad people 'turn another screw'?"

He had to reply, helplessly, "I do not think it is."

The sender before the same committee interpreted it as a request "to tighten up the machinery of their loose office." [3] Rice found out what the letter meant. "My rates were raised on that road over 50 per cent. in five days."

"Was it necessary to turn on more than one screw in that direction to put a stop to your business?"

[2] Testimony, Rice cases, Interstate Commerce Commission, Nos. 51-60, 1887, pp. 442-43.

[3] Trusts, Congress, 1888, pp. 524-30.

"One was sufficient." [4]

The rates to the combination remained unchanged. For five years —to 1886—they did not vary a mill. After the screw had been turned on, he who suggested it wrote to the offending merchants at Nashville, that if they persisted in bringing in this outside oil he would not only cut down the price of oil, but would enter into competition on all other articles sold in their grocery. He italicized this sentence: *"And certainly this competition will not be limited to coal-oil or any one article, and will not be limited to any one year."* [5] "Your co-operation or your life," says he.

"Have you not frequently, as a shipper of oil, taken part in the competition with grocers and others in other business than oil, in order to force them to buy oil?"

"Almost invariably I did that always." [6]

Rice fought out the fight at Nashville seven years, from 1880 to 1887; then, defeated, he had to shut up his agency there. That was "evacuation day" at Nashville. It was among his oldest agencies, he told Congress, "and it was shut out entirely last year on account of the discriminations. I cannot get in there." [7]

State inspection of oil and municipal ordinances about storage have been other "screws" that have been turned to get rid of competition. City councils passed ordinances forbidding oil in barrels to be stored, while allowing oil in tanks, which is very much more dangerous, as the records of oil fires and explosions show conclusively. His New Orleans agent wrote Rice concerning the manoeuvres of his pursuer; "He has been down here for some time, and has by his engineering, and in consequence of the city ordinances, cut me out of storage. As matters now stand, I would not be able to handle a single barrel of oil." [8] In Georgia the law was made so that the charge to the oil combination shipping in tank-cars was only half what it was to others who shipped in barrels. The State inspector's charge for oil in tanks was made 25 cents a barrel; for oil in barrels it was 50 cents a barrel. But as if that was not advantage enough, the inspector inspected the tanks at about two-thirds of their actual capacity. If an independent refiner sent 100 barrels of oil into the State, he would have to pay $50 for

[4] *Ibid.*, p. 620.
[5] *Ibid.*, pp. 534-36.
[6] *Ibid.*, p. 533.
[7] Trusts, Congress, 1888, p. 730.
[8] *Ibid.*, p. 733.

inspection, while the oil combination sending in the same would pay but 25 cents a barrel, and that on only 66 2/8 barrels, or $16 in all. This difference is a large commercial profit of itself, and would alone enable the one who received it to sell without loss at a price that would cripple all others. In this State the chief inspector had the power to appoint inspectors for the towns. He would name them only for the larger places, where the combination had storage tanks. This prevented independent refiners from shipping directly to the smaller markets in barrels, as they could not be inspected there, and if not inspected could not be sold.[9] All these manoeuvres of inspection helped to force the people to buy of only one dealer, to take what he supplied, and pay what he demanded. Why should an official appointed by the people, paid by them to protect them, thus use all his powers against them? Why?

"State whether you had not in your employ the State inspector of oil and gave him a salary," the Louisville representative of the combination was asked by Congress.

"Yes, sir." [10]

Throughout the country the people of the States have been influenced to pass inspection laws to protect themselves, as they supposed, from bad oil, with its danger of explosion. But these inspection laws prove generally to be special legislation in disguise, operating directly to deprive the people of the benefit of that competition which would be a self-acting inspection. They are useful only as an additional illustration of the extent to which government is being used as an active partner by great business interests. Meanwhile any effort of the people to use their own forces through governments to better their condition, as by the ownership of municipal gas-works, street-railways, or national railroads and telegraphs, is sung to sleep with the lullaby about government best, government least.

This second campaign had been a formidable affair—a worse was to follow; but it did not overcome the independent of Marietta. With all these odds against him, he made his way. Expelled from one place and another, like Memphis and Nashville, he found markets elsewhere. This was because the Southern people gave him market support along with their moral support. Co-operation of father and son and daughter made oil cheaper than the "sympatheti-

⁹ Trusts, Congress, 1888, p. 735.
¹⁰ Ibid., p. 535.

cal co-operation" opposing them, with its high salaries, idle refineries, and deadheads. Rice had to pay no dividends on "trust"
stock capitalized for fifteen times the value of the property. He did
not, like every one of the trustees, demand for himself an income
of millions a year from the consumer. He found margin enough
for survival, and even something more than survival, between the
cost of production and the market price. "In 1886 we were increasing our business very largely. Our rates were low enough so that
we could compete in the general Southern market." [11]

Upon this thrice-won prosperity fell now blow after blow from
the same hand which had struck so heavily twice before. From
1886 to the present moment Rice and his family have been kept
busier defending their right to live in business than in doing the
business itself. Their old enemy has come at them for the third
time, with every means of destruction that could be devised, from
highway exclusion to attacks upon private character, given currency by all the powerful means at his command. The game of
1886 was that of 1879, but with many improvements gained from
experience and progress of desire. His rates were doubled, sometimes almost tripled; in some cases as much as 333 per cent. Rates
to his adversary were not raised at all. The raise was secret. Suspect-
ing something wrong, he called on the railroad officer July 13th,
and asked what rates were going to be. The latter replied that he
"had not the list made out." But the next day he sent it in full
to the combination. Rice could not get them until August 23d,
six weeks later, and then not all of them. As in 1879 the new tariff
was arranged at a conference with the favored shippers.[12]

Rice shows that in some cases these discriminations made him
pay four times as much freight, gallon for gallon, as the monopoly.
The differences against him were so great that even the self-con-
tained Interstate Commerce Commission has to call them "a vast
discrepancy." [13] The power that pursued him manoeuvred against
him, as if it were one track, all the railroads from Pennsylvania to
Florida, from Ohio to Lake Superior and the Pacific coast.
"Through its representative the oil combination was called before
the Interstate Commerce Commission to explain its relation to this
'vast discrepancy.' "

"Your company pays full rates?"

[11] Trusts, Congress, 1888, p. 578.
[12] Trusts, Congress, 1888, pp. 579-80.
[13] Ibid., pp. 682-83.

"Pays the rates that I understand are the rates for everybody."

"Pays what are known as open rates?"

"Open rates; yes, sir." [14]

That the increase of rates in 1886, like that of 1879, was made by the railroads against Rice, under the direction of his trade enemy, is confirmed by the unwilling testimony of the latter's representative before Congress. "I know I have been asked just informally by railroad men once or twice as to what answer they should make. They said, Here is a man—Rice, for instance—writing us that you are getting a lower rate." He was asked if he knew any reason, legal or moral, why the Louisville and Nashville Railroad should select his firm as the sole people in the United States. "No, sir," the witness replied; but then added, recovering himself, "I think they did because we were at the front." [15] The railroads bring the people they prefer "to the front," and then, because they are "at the front," make them the "sole people."

Rice did not sleep under this new assault. He went to the Attorney-General of Ohio, and had those of the railroads which were Ohio corporations brought to judgment before the Supreme Court of Ohio, which revoked their action, and could, if it chose, have forfeited their charters. The Supreme Court found that these railroads had charged "discriminating rates," "strikingly excessive," which "tended to foster a monopoly," "actually excluded these competitors," "giving to the favored shippers absolute control." [16] Rice went to Cincinnati, to Louisville, to St. Louis, and Baltimore to see the officials of the railroads. He found that the roads to the South and West, which took his oil from the road which carried it out of Marietta, were willing to go back to the old rates if the connecting road would do so. But the general freight agent of that company would give him no satisfaction. He wrote, October 3d, to the president of the road over which he had done all his business for years. He got no answer. He wrote again October 11th, no answer; October 20th, no answer; November 14th, no answer. Rice had been paying this road nearly $10,000 a year for freight, sending all his oil over it. The road had used its rate-making power to hand over four-fifths of his business to another, but he has never

[14] Testimony, Rice cases, Interstate Commerce Commission, 1887, Nos. 51-60, p. 57.

[15] Trusts, Congress, 1888, pp. 529-32.

[16] Supreme Court of Ohio: the State, ex rel., vs. The Cincinnati, New Orleans and Texas Pacific Railway Company. The State, ex rel., vs. The Cincinnati, Washington and Baltimore Railway Company, 47 Ohio State Reports, p. 130.

been able to get so much as a formal acknowledgment of the receipt of his letters to the head of the road, asking that his petitions for restoration of his rights on the highway be considered. A part only of the letters and telegrams which he sent during these years—to get rates, to have his cars moved, to rectify unequal charges, to receive the same facilities and treatment others got—fill pages of close print in the Trust Report of the Congressional Committee of Manufactures of 1888.

Rice, badly shattered, still sought and managed to find a few long-way-around routes. He presented to Congress in 1888 a table showing how he still managed to get to some of his markets. To Birmingham, Alabama—the direct route of 685 miles, as well as the Baltimore and Ohio, being closed to him—he shipped over seven different railroads forward and backward 1155 miles. The rates of all these roads added together made only $2.10 a barrel instead of $2.66, to which the shorter line had raised its price, for the purpose, as this comparison shows, not of getting revenue, but of cutting it off. To get into Nashville he had to go around 805 miles over five different lines instead of 502 miles, as usual, and still had a rate of $1.28 instead of $1.60.

It was not enough to fix his rates at double what others paid. All kinds of mistakes were made about his shipments. Again and again these mistakes were repeated; nor were they, the Interstate Commerce Commission shows, corrected when pointed out.[17] One of the stock excuses made by railroad managers for giving preferential rates to their favorites is that they are the "largest shippers," and, consequently, "entitled to a wholesale rate." But when Rice was the largest shipper, as he was at New Orleans, they forgot to give him the benefit of this "principle." When Rice wrote, asking if a lower rate was not being made, the railroad agent replied: "Let me repeat that the rates furnished you are just as low as furnished anybody else." "This lacks accuracy," is the comment of the Interstate Commerce Commission.

Wishing to know if the Louisville and Nashville would unite with other roads in making through rates to him, Rice asked the question of its freight agent. He replied: "I do not see that it is any of your business." "It was undoubtedly his business," the Interstate Commerce Commission says, sharply; "and his inquiry on the subject was not wanting either in civility or propriety." When

<hr/>

[17] Trusts, Congress, 1888, pp. 586, 676. Testimony, Rice cases, Interstate Commerce Commission, Nos. 51-60, 1887, pp. 391-92.

Rice asked the same road for rates, the officials refused to give
them to him, and persisted in their refusal.[18] Like Vanderbilt before the New York Legislative Committee, they seemed to think
excuses to shippers were a substitute for transportation, and evidently thought they had done more than their duty in answering
Rice's letters. But as the Commission dryly observes, their answers
to Rice's letters did not relieve him of the injurious consequences.
In attempting to explain these things to the Interstate Commerce
Commission, the agent of the railroad said:

"If I have not made myself clear, I—"

"You have not," one of the Commission interrupted.[19]

The refusal to give Rice these rates was an "illegal refusal," the
Commission decided; "the obligation to give the rates . . . was
plain and unquestionable." This general freight agent was sum-
moned by Congress to tell whether or not lower rates had been
made to the oil combination than to their competitors. He refused
to produce the books and papers called for by the subpoena. He
had been ordered by the vice-president of the road, he said, to
refuse. He declined to answer the questions of the committee. Recalled, he finally admitted the truth: "We gave them lower
rates in some instances." [20]

Rice took to the water whenever he could, as hunted animals do.
The Ohio, Mississippi, Tennessee, Missouri were public highways
that had not been made private property, with general agents or
presidents to say "No" when asked permission to travel over them.
He began to ship by river. The chairman of the Committee of
Commerce rose in his seat in Congress to present favorably a bill
to make it illegal to ship oil of less than 150 degrees fire-test on
the passenger boats of inland waters. The reason ostentatiously
given was public safety. But, as was at once pointed out in the
press, the public safety required no such law. The test proposed
was far above the requirement of safety. No State in its inspection
laws stipulated for so high a test. Most of the States were satisfied
with oil of 110 degrees fire-test; a few, like Ohio, went as high as
120 degrees. All but a very small proportion of the oil sent to
Europe was only 110 degrees fire-test. The steamboat men did
not want the law, and were all against it. There was no demand
from the travelling public for such legislation. General Warner,

[18] Trusts, Congress, 1888, pp. 676-77.
[19] Rice cases, Nos. 51-60, 1887, p. 119.
[20] Trusts, Congress, 1880, p. 520.

member of Congress, said, in opposing the bill: "Petroleum which will stand a fire-test of 110 degrees is safer than baled cotton or baled hay, and as safe as whiskey or turpentine to be carried on steamers. What is the object, then? There can be but one, and I may as well assert it here, although I make no imputation whatever upon the Committee of Commerce, or any member of it. It will put the whole carrying trade of refined petroleum into the hands of the railroads and under the control of . . . a monopoly which has the whole carrying trade in the oil business on railroads, and they will make it as impossible for refiners to exist along the lakes and the Ohio River as it is impossible for them now to exist on any of the railroads of the country." Why the trust, though it was the greatest shipper, should seek to close up channels of cheapness like the waterways was plain enough. They were highways where privilege was impossible. With its competitors shut off the railroads by privilege, and off the rivers by law, it would be competition proof.

The United States authorities, too, moved against Rice, responsive to the same "pull" that made jumping-jacks for monopoly out of committees of commerce and railway kings. When the Mississippi River steamer *U.P. Schenck* arrived at Vicksburg with 56 barrels of independent oil, the United States marshal came on board to serve a process summoning the officers and owners to answer to the charge of an alleged violation of law. Several steamboats were similarly "libelled."

"We were threatened a great many times," the representative of the steamboat company told Congress.[21] The steamboat men were put to great expense and without proper cause. When the cases came to trial they were completely cleared in every instance. But the prosecution had done its work of harassing competition. The success of the campaign of 1879 in Ohio was now repeated over a wider field. The attack of 1886, "in a period of five months," Rice said before Congress, "shut up fourteen of my agencies out of twenty-four, and reduced the towns we had been selling in from seventy-three to thirty-four." [22] This was a loss in one year of 79 per cent, or about four-fifths of his business.

[21] Trusts, Congress, 1880, pp. 410-11.
[22] Trusts, Congress, 1888, p. 599.

XVII

In the Interest of All

How history is made! One of the reasons given by the solicitor of the oil trust[1] for its success is its use of the tank-car with the obvious inference that its would-be competitors had no such enterprise. And Peckham, in his valuable and usually correct "Census Report on Petroleum," in 1885, says that the railroads require shippers to use tank-cars! [2]

Determined to keep in the field and to have tank-cars, if tank-cars were so popular with the railroad officials, Rice went to the leading manufacturers to have some built. He found they were glad to get his contract. After making arrangements at considerable trouble and expense to build him the cars, they telegraphed him that they had to give it up. Bankers, who had promised to advance them money on the security of the cars, backed out "on account of some supposed controversy which they claim you have had with the Standard Oil Company and various railroads in the West. They feared you could not use these cars to advantage if the railroads should be hostile to your interests." [3]

Through the all-pervading system of espionage, to which cities[4] as well as individuals were subject, his plans had been discovered and thwarted. The espionage over shipments provided for by the South Improvement scheme has now extended to business between manufacturer and manufacturer. Why should it stop at unsealing private correspondence in the post-office in the European style, and

[1] *Combinations*, by S. C. T. Dodd, p. 29.
[2] "Petroleum and Its Products," by S. F. Peckham, U.S. Census, 1885, p. 92.
[3] Trusts, Congress, 1888, p. 614.
[4] See ch. xxiv

making its contents known to those who need the information for the protection of their rights to the control of the markets?

Rice, who was nothing if not indomitable, finally got ten cars from the Harrisburg works. But this supply was entirely inadequate, and he had to continue doing the bulk of his business in barrels. What a devil's tattoo the railroad men beat on these barrels of his! They made him pay full tariff rates on every pound weight of the oil and of the barrel, but they hauled free the iron tanks, which were the barrels of his rivals, and also gave them free the use of the flat-cars on which the tanks were carried.[5] Hauling the tanks free, on trucks furnished free, was not enough. The railroads hauled free of all charge a large part, often more than half, of the oil put into the tanks. In the exact phrase of the Interstate Commerce Commission, they made out their bills for freight to the oil combination "regardless of quantity." This is called "blind-billing."

Of the 3000 tank-cars of the combination only two carried as little as 20,000 pounds; according to the official figures there were hundreds carrying more than 30,000 pounds, and the weight ran up to 44,250 pounds, but they were shipped at 20,000.[6] A statement put in evidence showed that shipments in tank-cars actually weighing 1,637,190 pounds had been given to the roads by the combination as weighing only 1,192,655 pounds. Cars whose loads weighed 44,250, 43,700, 43,500, 36,550 pounds were shipped as having on board only 20,000 pounds. At this rate more than one-quarter of the transportation was stolen.

The stockholders of the road were paying an expensive staff of inspectors to detect attempts of shippers to put more in their cars than they paid for, but these shippers paid for three car-loads and shipped from four to six regularly, and were never called to account. This "blind-billing," the Commission said, was "specially oppressive." It had been mutually agreed among them, and given out to the public, "that tank-cars shall be taken at actual weight." [7]

The representative of the combination was called as a witness before the Interstate Commerce Commission. "We pay for exactly what is put in the tanks," [8] he testified. "In fact, this was never

<hr />

[5] Testimony, Rice cases, Interstate Commerce Commission, Nos. 51-60, 1887, p. 144.

[6] Trusts, Congress, 1888, pp. 587, 675, 680. Rice cases, Nos. 51-60, 1887, pp. 487-88. For similar preferences to the palace cattle-car companies, see report on "Meat Products," United States Senate, 1890, p. 18.

[7] Rice cases, Nos. 51-60, 1887, p. 477.

[8] *Ibid.*, p. 47.

done," says the Commission.[9] Even the railroad officials, who could go any length in "blind-billing" for him, could not "go it blind" on the witness-stand to the extent of supporting such a statement. "Our price per tank-car was not based on any capacity or weight; they have been made simply per tank-car." [10]

"What, generally, is the object of false billing?"

"I suppose to beat the railroad company." [11]

In defence of the discrimination against the barrel shippers, a great deal has been made of danger from fire, damage to cars from leakage, and trouble of handling in the case of barrel shipments, but the best expert opinion which the Interstate Commerce Commission could get went against all these plausible pretences.[12] The manager of the tank line on the Pennsylvania roads showed that the risks were least when the transportation was in barrels. Another reason given for the lower rates on tanks was that they returned loaded with turpentine and cotton-seed oil from the South; but, as the Interstate Commerce Commission shows, this traffic was taken at rates so astonishingly low that it was of little profit;[13] and the commissioner of the Southern Railway and Steamship Association informed the Commission that the return freight business in cotton alone, brought back by the box-cars, to say nothing of other freight, was worth more than these back-loads of turpentine in the tank-cars.[14] It was, consequently, the box-car in which barrel shipments were made, and not the tanks, on which the railroad men should have given a better rate, according to their own reasoning. Turpentine and cottonseed oil are worth three or four times more than kerosene, and it costs no more, no less, to haul one than the other; but the railroads would carry the cotton-seed oil and turpentine for one-third or one-fourth the rate they charged for kerosene. The Commission could not understand why the rates given by the roads on these back-loads of turpentine and cotton-seed oil were so low. "This charge, for some reason not satisfactorily explained to the Commission, is made astonishingly low when compared with the charge made upon petroleum, although the cotton-seed oil is much the more valuable article." [15]

[9] Trusts, Congress, 1888, p. 675.
[10] Rice cases, Nos. 51-60, 1887, pp. 108-109.
[11] Ibid., p. 120.
[12] See ch. xi.
[13] Trusts, Congress, 1888, p. 674.
[14] Rice cases, Nos. 51-60, 1887, p. 480.
[15] Trusts, Congress, 1888, p. 674.

The newspapers of the South have contained many items of news indicating that the men who have made the oil markets theirs have similarly appropriated the best of the turpentine trade, but nothing is known through adjudicated testimony. The trustees of oil have always denied that there was any connection between them and the Cotton-seed Oil Trust, although the latter shipped its product in the oil trust's cars. The reasons, therefore, for the "extraordinarily low" rates made on the turpentine and cotton-seed oil shipped North in its tank-cars must remain, until further developments, where the Commission leaves it—"not satisfactorily explained." The railroads said they made the rates low for tanks because of the enticing prospects of these back-loads, in which there was no profit to speak of; but they extended these special rates to points from which there was no such back-loading.[16] Rice saw how the cost of sending his oil South could be reduced by bringing back-loads of turpentine at these "astonishingly low" rates. He found there was still turpentine in the South he could buy; but the railroads would not so much as answer his application for rates.

"They absolutely refused."

"Was this refusal since the Interstate Commerce decision in your case?"

"Yes, sir; since that decision." [17]

It might have been thought this would have been enough—hauling the tank itself free; furnishing the flat-cars free for many tanks; carrying free a quarter to a half, "or more." But there was more than this. The railroads paid the combination for putting its tank-cars on their lines. For every mile these cars were hauled, loaded or empty, the roads paid it a mileage varying from $\frac{3}{4}$ to $1\frac{1}{2}$ cents. This mileage was of itself a handsome revenue, enough to pay a profit of 6 per cent. on its investment in the cars. But when Rice asked what the railroads would charge him for hauling back his empty tank-cars, he was not told that he would be paid for their use, as others were. He was told that he would be charged "generally a cent and a half a mile," or, "we make the usual mileage charge on return of empty tanks." "This last statement," the Interstate Commerce Commissioners say, "was not warranted by the facts." [18] The vessel which contains the oil of the combination "receives a hire coming and going," Mr. Rice's lawyer said before

[16] Trusts, Congress, 1888, pp. 531-33.
[17] Ibid., pp. 646-47.
[18] Trusts, Congress, 1888, pp. 668-85.

the Committee of Congress on Commerce; "that which contains
Rice's oil pays a tax." When Rice tried to sell his oil on the Pacific
coast he found that if he shipped in tank-cars he would have to
pay $95 to bring the empty car back, which others got back free.
The representative of the oil combination was questioned about
all this by the Interstate Commerce Commission.

"Are you allowed mileage on tank-cars?"

"No, sir."

"Neither way?"

"Neither way." [19]

But the railroad officials again could not "blind-bill" him as far
as this. Asked what mileage they paid him, they replied:

"Three-quarters of a cent a mile." [20]

When the freight agents who did these queer things at the expense of their employers—*i.e.*, their proper employers, the stockholders—were put on the stand before the Interstate Commerce
Commission to explain, they cut a sorry figure. "It was an over-
sight," "a mistake," said one. Another could only ring confused
changes on "I think it is an error . . . I cannot tell why that is
so . . . It is simply an error . . . I cannot tell." [21] There were
never any errors, suppositions, oversights for Rice.[22] Referring to
this, the Commission says, caustically:

"The remarkable thing about the matter is that so many of
these defendants should make the same mistake—a mistake, too,
that it was antecedently so improbable any of them would make.
The Louisville and Nashville, the Cincinnati, New Orleans and
Texas Pacific, the Newport News and Mississippi Valley, and the
Illinois Central companies are all found giving out the same erroneous information, and no one of them can tell how or why it
happened to be done, much less how so many could contempo-
raneously, in dealing with the same subject, fall into so strange an
error. It is to be noted, too, that it is not a subordinate agent or
servant who makes the mistake in any instance, but it is the man
at the head of the traffic department, and whose knowledge on
the subject any inquirer would have a right to assume must be
accurate. In no case is the error excused." [23]

[19] Rice cases, Nos. 51-60, p. 65.
[20] *Ibid.*, p. 131.
[21] *Ibid.*, pp. 128-29, 143-47, 239.
[22] Rice cases, Nos. 51-60, p. 109. Trusts, Congress, 1888, pp. 675-76.
[23] Trusts, Congress, 1888, p. 688.

The cases in which Rice prosecuted the railroads before the Interstate Commerce Commission are among the most important that have been tried by the Commission. The charges made by Rice were conclusively proved, except as to some minor roads and circumstances. The Commission declared the rates that were charged him to be illegal and unjust, and a discrimination that must be stopped. It ordered the roads to discontinue using their power as common carriers to carry Rice's property into the possession of a rival. "The conclusion is irresistible that the rate sheets were not considerately made with a view to relative justice." [24]

The facts of these discriminations—"unjust," "illegal," and "abhorrent"—are on the records as judicially and finally determined. But one of the combination said before the Pennsylvania Legislature, at Harrisburg, as reported in the Harrisburg *Patriot*, February 19, 1891:

> I say to you all, in good faith, that since the passage of the Interstate Commerce law, and the introduction of that system, we have never taken a rebate. I mean we have taken no advantage over what any other shipper can get. I make the statement broadly, and I challenge the statement to the very utmost, and will pay the expenses of any litigation undertaken to try it.

When it was found that this practice of charging the preferred shipper for only 20,000 pounds when it shipped 25,000, 30,000, 40,000 or 44,000, was going to be investigated by the Interstate Commerce Commission, there were intellects ready to meet the emergency. A pot of paint and a paint brush furnished the shield of righteousness. Each car being known by its number, and only by its number, all the old numbers of the 3000 tank-cars of the oil trust were painted out, and new numbers painted on. Whether its mighty men left their luxurious palaces in New York, and stole about in person after dark, each with paint-pot and brush, or whether they asked employés to do such work, the evidence does not state. The device was simple, but it did. Rice was suing for his rights to use the highways before the Interstate Commerce Commission, and before the Supreme Court of Ohio, through the Attorney-General of the State, who had found the matter of sufficient importance to use his official power to institute suits in *quo-warranto* against two railroads. It was necessary that evidence should be forthcoming in these suits to prove what his rate was in

[24] Trusts, Congress, 1888, p. 689.

comparison with the others. The only way this could be done was by comparing the actual size of the cars with the size given in the freight bills, or manifests. The cars are known in the bills only by their numbers, and without its number no car could be identified. The report of Congress reprints the following from the testimony of the representative of the trust before the Interstate Commerce Commission:

"Has there recently been any general change in the numbering of the cars?"

"Yes, sir; there has been quite a general renumbering, repainting, and overhauling."

"When did that change take place?"

"I think it was commenced some time in July; it may have been iater."

The result of that renumbering made it practically impossible to identify any car as connected with any shipment made before that time. The cars were there, looking as fresh and innocent as good men who have donned robes of spotless white earned by the payment of generous pew-rent. The cars showed even to the unassisted eye, as the Interstate Commerce Commission said, how much larger they were than was pretended. There were still the accounts of the railroads, showing that these cars had been "blind-billed" as containing only 20,000 pounds, but the cars mentioned in the manifesto could no longer be identified with the cars on the tracks. The sin of "blind-billing" was washed out in paint. Rice went to the Interstate Commerce Commission with his complaint in this case in July. Immediately the repainting and renumbering took place. "It was commenced some time in July; it may have been later." [25]

In such cases time is money, and more. "Seest thou a man diligent in business, he shall stand before kings. He shall not stand before mean men."

When the amendment of the Interstate Commerce law was before Congress in 1889, eminent counsel were employed by Rice to explain the defects of the law to the committees, and petitions to Congress through his instrumentality were circulated all over the country, and numerously signed. Though a poor man, who could ill afford it, he gave time and money and attention, frequently spending weeks at Washington, discussing the subject with mem-

[25] Trusts, Congress, 1888, pp. 598-99. Testimony, Rice cases, Nos. 51-60, 1887, p. 28.

bers, and presenting petitions. The act was amended in partial accordance with these petitions and recommendations.

To obtain the elementary right of a stockholder, never withheld in the course of ordinary business—to vote and receive dividends on stock in the oil trust which the trustees had sold and he had bought in the open market—Rice had to sue through all the New York courts from 1888 to 1892. The Court of Appeals decided that there had been no lawful reason for the denial of his rights, and ordered that they be accorded him. This was another barren victory. The trust had meanwhile ostensibly been dissolved; but the dissolution has every appearance of being like that of its progenitor, the South Improvement Company, a dissolution "in name" only; not in reality. In place of the old trust certificates listed on the New York Stock Exchange, new certificates have been issued which were selling in the spring of 1894 at about the same quotation as the former ones.

In this case the trust asked the New York courts to deny Rice his rights because he had in other matters, and as to other parties, appealed to other courts. His other suits had been against the railroads, not against the oil combination. He acted on the defensive, and went into court only to save himself from commercial strangulation. In all of them that went to trial he was successful, with but one or two exceptions. He was so successful that even the judges who heard his case and decided in his favor were moved to outbursts of unaffected indignation on the bench. The only result aimed at or procured was that the courts decreed that these common carriers must in the future give this citizen his legal rights on the railways; not that he must have the same rates as his opponent, but only that the difference in their favor shall not be "excessive," "illegal," "unjust."

Because of this attempt to secure the fair use of the highways side by side with it, the trust pleaded in the Supreme Court of New York that his appeal to courts as a shipper was a reason why the courts should withhold his rights as a stockholder.

In making this plea the trustees described themselves as having been for years persecuted by the independent of Marietta, and moistened the dry pages of their legal pleadings with appeals for the sympathy of the courts and the public. He has "diligently and persistently sought to become acquainted with" our "methods of business and private affairs"; "he has used efforts to injure" our "business"; "he is attempting to harass, injure, and annoy" us; "he

has ever since . . . 1876, when he first engaged in business, . . .
maintained a hostile attitude, and been engaged in hostile transactions and proceedings against" us, . . . "for the purpose of injuring" us and our "business"; he "has been uninterruptedly
prosecuting . . . a series of litigations . . . in the courts, as well as
before the Interstate Commerce Commission, and before an investigating committee of Congress . . . for the purpose of harassing
and annoying us." [26] And when in 1891 Rice was appealing to the
Attorney-General of New York to bring suit in the name of the
State against the oil combination in New York, like that which
had been successfully brought in Ohio, he was publicly stigmatized
in court as a "black-mailer" because he had once named a price
at which he was willing to sell his refinery and quit. So the
citizens of Nashville were called black-mailers for competing, and
the citizens of Buffalo for bringing a criminal conspiracy to justice.

It is this dancing attendance upon State legislatures, courts, attorney-generals, Congress, the Interstate Commerce Commission, as
shown in this recital, which the modern American business man
must add to Thrift, Industry, and Sobriety as a condition of survival.

[26] Rice vs. Standard Oil Trust. New York Court of Appeals—Case on Appeal,
1888.

XXIII

Freedom of the City

Towns, like men, stamp themselves with marked traits. Toledo had an individuality which showed itself from the start. Its leading men clubbed together and borrowed money as early as 1832 to build one of the first railroads constructed west of the Alleghanies —the Erie and Kalamazoo, to connect Toledo and Adrian. When, in 1845, the steamboats on the lakes formed a combination, and discriminated against Toledo, the city through its council refused to submit, and appropriated $10,000 to get an independent boat to Buffalo. The city appropriated its credit and revenues to other important and costly enterprises, including four railroads, to keep it clear of the cruel mercies of private ownership of the highways. In 1889 it expended $200,000 to secure direct railway connections with the Pennsylvania and the Baltimore and Ohio railways for competition in rates with the Lake Shore Railroad.

As it had been authorized to do so by the State, the City Council of Toledo, April 29, 1889, ordered gas bonds to the amount of $75,000 sold, that work on the city pipe line might begin. Before proceeding with the enterprise confided to them, the natural-gas trustees gave the private companies an opportunity to save themselves from the competition of the city. They asked them in writing if they would agree to furnish gas cheaply for a term of years, or if they would sell their entire plant to the city? They did this, as they express it, as "an honorable effort . . . to obtain cheaper gas without unnecessary expenditure, and without injury to established right." After a delay of nearly a month a reply was received, refusing to enter into negotiations either for a reduction of charges or for the sale of the private plants to the city. The trustees then asked for a personal interview, but this was refused. Then when the city began preparations to sell its bonds, a cannonade was opened on it in the courts, the money-market, the gasfields, the city government, the press, among the citizens, and everywhere. Injunctions were applied for in three courts, unsuccessfully in all instances. No injunction was ever granted in these or any other of the many suits brought for the purpose of enjoining the sale of the bonds. Courts will usually grant temporary injunctions awaiting a hearing on the merits when complainants will enter into ample bonds and indemnify defendants. But the parties instigating this litigation would not put up the necessary bonds. They thus could smirch the bonds without incurring any personal liability in so doing.

An expensive array of lawyers was sent before the United States courts to prevent the issue of the bonds on the ground that they were illegal, and the law under which they we:e issued unconstitutional. The principle involved had been frequently discussed and always upheld both by the Supreme Court of Ohio and the Supreme Court of the United States.[1]

"Does not your argument appear to be in conflict with the views of the Supreme Court of Ohio and the Supreme Court of the United States?" the judge asked. The counsel for the gas companies responded in substance: "If so, then so much the worse for the views of those courts."

As it was through the suffrage that the people of Toledo were able to do this, the attack was widened from an attack on the enterprise to one upon the sovereignty of the citizens which made it possible. "Everybody votes in Ohio—in fact, too many people," said the lawyer who applied for an injunction against Toledo. If he had his way, he declared, there would be fewer voters, and he stigmatized the arguments of Toledo as those of John Most, the communist.

"Unquestionably," decided Judge Jackson, "the Legislature may authorize a city to furnish light, or facilities for transportation, or water to its citizens, with or without cost, as the Legislature or city may determine. . . . Since the decision in Sharpless vs. Philadelphia it is no longer an open question whether municipalities may engage in enterprises such as the one contemplated by the act in question in this case. The act of January 22, 1889, authorizing the city of Toledo to issue bonds for natural-gas purposes, is

---

[1] State, ex rel., vs. City of Toledo, 48th Ohio State Reports, p. 112.

clearly within the general scope of legislative power, is for a public use and purpose, and is not in contravention of any of the provisions of the constitution. The court being of the opinion that the legislation is valid, it follows, of course, that the injunction applied for must be refused." [2] When the news of Judge Jackson's decision was telegraphed to Toledo nothing less than the booming of cannon would express the joy of the citizens. They sent this message to the just judge: "One hundred guns were fired to-night by the citizens of Toledo in honor of your righteous decision to-day." Judge Jackson again upheld the bonds at Toledo, January 14, 1890, when he again dismissed the case against the city "for want of equity, at cost of complainants."

August 26, 1889, after a decision in the United States courts that there was no ground on which to object to the issue of the bonds, the City Council voted the issue of the remaining $675,000.

The only morning paper—an able advocate of the city pipe line—suddenly changed owners and opinions. Among its new directors were two of the lawyers of the trust opposing the city, a director in one of its companies, and, besides them, the manager, a contract editor from Pennsylvania. His sole conspicuity there had been won in turning against the people of the oil regions a paper which had been their stanchest defender. This Toledo daily, in its espousal of the cause of the city, had been firing hot shot like this against the oil combination: "It wants a monopoly of the natural-gas business. This is what it is driving at." Under its new management it roared like a sucking dove, thus: "It is fashionable with demagogues and men who are not capable of appreciating the worth of brains in business to howl against it"—the oil combination —"as a grasping, grinding monopoly." Just after the people had decided in favor of the pipe line, and only a few days before it changed owners, it had said: "All manner of influences were brought to bear to defeat this proposition. . . . All the plausible falsehoods that could be invented, and all the money that could be used, were industriously employed, but the people saw the situation in its true light, and the majority voted right." It now made the defeat of the city's pipe line the chief aim of its endeavors. In this work "no rule or principle recognized in decent journalism was respected."

In all the history of Toledo no interest on its bonds had ever been defaulted or delayed; no principal ever unpaid at maturity.

[2] *Federal Court Reporter*, vol. xxxix., pp. 651-54.

The city was prosperous, its growth steady; its debt growing less year by year in proportion to its population and wealth. Its bonds ranked among the choicest investments, and commanded a premium in the money-market.[3] But the credit and fair fame of the city were now overwhelmed with wholesale vituperation by this paper, and others elsewhere under similar control. Articles were carefully prepared for this purpose by skilled writers. These were then copied from one newspaper to another. By some arrangement insertion was obtained for them in financial journals in New York and in London, and in other foreign capitals. The Toledo organ declared that Toledo was an unsafe place for the investment of capital in any form. Its public affairs were said to be run by a set of "demagogues and speculators," whose administration was "piratical mob rule." The city pipe line was a "monstrous job," and the men who favored it were "a gang of throttlers and ravenous wolves." They were "blatant demagogues, who made great pretence of advancing the city's interest, but whose real aim is to enrich themselves at public expense." The bonds which had been issued in due form by special authority of the Legislature, ratified by a vote of more than three-fifths of the citizens, and declared to be valid by the United States Court, were described as "chromos," "worthless rags," "bad medicine," "disfigured securities," "like rotten eggs, highly odorous goods," "but few persons at most can be found ignorant enough to buy them."

The Mayor, City Auditor, Board of Natural Gas Trustees, united with a citizens' committee of the Board of Trade in a plan to promote the sale of the bonds direct to the people of Toledo through a financial institution of the highest standing. This action the paper described as "a scheme for gulling simples," "a blind pool," "an unpatented financial deadfall"; compared it with "gambling, pool-playing, and lottery selling." These grave charges were widely circulated throughout the country. Bankers and capitalists in other cities who received them had no means of knowing that they were not what they pretended to be—the honest if uncouth utterances of an independent press chastising the follies of its own constituency. Newspapers which supported the city's project were assailed as ruthlessly as the community and citizens. The *Blade* was constantly referred to as "The Bladder." Another journal was given a nickname too vulgar to be printed here. One of the most prominent journals of Ohio was punished by the following para-

[3] City of Toledo and Its Natural Gas Bonds, p. 3.

graph, which is a fair sample of the literary style of monopoly: "That aged, acidulous addlepate, the monkey-eyed, monkey-browed monogram of sarcasm, and spider-shanked, pigeon-witted public scold, Majah Bilgewater Bickham, and his backbiting, black-mailing, patent-medicine directory, the *Journal*."

An old journalist and honorable citizen who wrote over his initials, "C.W.," a series of able and dignified letters in the *Blade*, which had a great influence in the formation of public opinion in favor of the pipe line, was assailed with "brutal falsifier," "hoary old reprobate," "senile old liar." Caricatures were published depicting the buyers of the bonds as "simple greens." When the County Court of Lucas County, following the United States Court, sustained the bonds on their merits, and did so on every point in question, because, as the judge stated, "the equities of the case are with the defendants," the organ falsely stated that judgment for the city was given "because the merits of the case are involved in a higher court." When a capitalist of New York, who had been an investor in the bonds of Toledo and a taxpayer there for twenty-five years—one of the streets of the city was named for him —bought $10,000 of the city pipe-line bonds, the paper attacked him by name in an article headed "Bunco Game," charging him with being a party to a bunco game in connection with "public till-tappers" for "roping Toledo citizens into buying doubtful securities." When the Sinking Fund Commissioners of Toledo very properly invested some of the city's money in the gas bonds, they were held up by name as "public till-tappers," "menials" of a "hungry horde" of "boodle politicians," accomplices of "plunderers of the public treasury," unable to withstand "the brutal threats and snaky entreaties of the corrupt gas ring." For one of the associate editors the position of Deputy State Inspector of Oil was obtained—an appointment which cost the Governor who made it many votes in the next election, and did much to defeat him. Such an appointment might give a versatile employé the chance to do double duty: as editor to brand as bad good men who could not be bought, and as inspector to brand as good bad oil for sale.[4]

One of the means taken to defeat the pipe line was the publication of very discouraging accounts of the "failure" at Indianapolis, where the citizens had refused to give a natural-gas company belonging to the oil trust the franchise it demanded, and, forming an anti-monopoly trust, had undertaken to supply themselves. Some

[4] See ch. xxix.

"influence" prevented the Common Council of Toledo from sending a committee to Indianapolis to investigate. A public-spirited
citizen, prominent and successful in business, came forward, and
at his own expense secured a full and accurate account of the
experience of Indianapolis for the city. This proved that the people were getting their fuel gas at less than one-half what Toledo
was paying. The contest against giving the Indianapolis franchise
to a corporation of the trust had been a sharp one. Its success
was due to the middle classes and the working-men, who stood
together for freedom, incorruptible by all the powerful influences
employed. "We will burn soft coal all our lives," one of their
leaders told the Toledo committee, "rather than put ourselves in
the power of such men."

In Indiana the Legislature meets only once in two years, and
when this issue arose had adjourned, and would not meet again
for a year. The people, not being able to get authority for a
municipal gas pipe line, went to work by voluntary cooperation.
Every voting precinct in the city was organized and canvassed for
the capital needed. The shares were $25 each, and they were
bought up so rapidly that the entire amount—$550,000—was sub-
scribed in sixteen days by 4700 persons, without a cent of cost
to the city. When subscriptions to the amount of $550,000 had
been raised, $600,000 more was borrowed on certificates of indebted-
ness.

Gas lands were bought and 200 miles of pipe lines laid, all at a
cost of about $1,200,000. The income in one year, during a part
of which the system was still under construction, was $349,347. In
the first year of complete operations the Indianapolis people's
trust paid off $90,000 of the principal. The income for the year
ending October 31, 1892, was $483,258.21, and the bonded debt
has been paid. The stock, since January 1, 1893, has been paying
dividends at the rate of 8 per cent. a year.

A year after the inauguration of the Indianapolis movement a
committee of the citizens at Dayton, who had risen against the extortionate prices charged them, investigated the condition of affairs at Indianapolis. They reported that Indianapolis had paid
$200,000 on its bonded debt, and was getting ready to pay as much
more. The Consumers' Trust supplied between 10,000 and 11,000
consumers, and spent $1,000,000 less than the Dayton private com-
pany spent to supply 3000 fewer consumers. The annual charge at
Dayton was $54.80; at Indianapolis only $26.80—less than half.

When facts like these were brought out, to the demolition of the fictions circulated in Toledo, the answer was characteristic. The "organ" could not deny the statements, but it fell upon the citizen through whose generosity the information had been got for the people, and assailed his private character in articles which, one of the daily papers declared, editorially, "would almost, if not quite, justify him in shooting their author on sight."

This newspaper charged the city natural-gas trustees with being "rotten to the core," and with every variation of phrase possible to its exuberant rhetoric sounded the changes upon their official career as a "big steal," "fostered by deception, falsehood, and skull-duggery." It sought to intimidate the Legislature and the courts when they failed to enact or construe laws against the people. It said: "Law-makers, judges, and others may feel the force of this element when the proper time comes and political preferment is sought."

It was money in pocket that facts like those of the experience of Indianapolis, Detroit, and other places should not be made known. Even ideas must not be allowed to reach the public mind. Professor Henry C. Adams, the well-known political economist, lectured in Toledo during this contest, in a University Extension Course, on "Public Commissions Considered as the Conservative Solution of the Monopoly Problem." The "organ" gave a synopsis of the lecturer's views, which is printed herewith in parallel columns, with a synopsis of what Mr. Adams really said, as revised by himself:

WHAT THE ORGAN OF MONOPOLY REPORTED.	WHAT THE LECTURER REALLY SAID.
The lecturer made reference to Toledo as an unfavorable place to discuss the matter of municipal control of quasi-public business and competition of municipalities with private corporations. But he deprecated anything in that line. He did not mention particular instances, but broadly condemned the policy pursued by this city in matters of this kind, and his remarks had a visible effect on his audience. He considered municipal control of business enterprises the worst form	Professor Adams thought the solution of the monopoly problem must be found either in public control or in public ownership. He advocated public control, and held that the State and Federal railroad commissions should have a fair trial, that their hands should be strengthened by further and adequate legislation. He entertained the hope that this control and regulation would ultimately protect the interests of the public in a satisfactory manner. He was willing to admit, however, if this

of monopoly, as they began by having the unfair advantage of the law-making power, and the tendency to corruption was greater than when individual enterprises were asking privileges. The audience was much pleased with the lecturer.

effort to secure the needed public control by the aid of commissions and legislation should fail, then public ownership was the only remaining solution. He held that in local monopolies it may still be wise to try the experiment of public control by aid of commissions. He said, however, that if anything should be owned and controlled by and for the people it would be street-railroads, gas and water works. He admonished his audience not to be misled by the argument that municipal ownership would be dangerous because of undue political influence, for the local monopolies under private ownership were already in politics, and in a most dangerous manner. He observed facetiously that he hesitated to discuss the question of municipal control or ownership before a Toledo audience.

From the control of the markets to the control of the minds of a people—this is the line of march.

So direct, persistent, and bold were the charges of corruptions rung day after day by this journal against all the officials concerned in the city gas enterprise that some people began to believe there must be truth in them. But when the community at last turned upon its maligners, and the grand-jury brought indictments against the active manager of the paper and his chief assistant for criminal libel upon the city's natural-gas trustees, the whole structure of their falsehood went down at a breath. They had no defence whatever. They made no attempt to justify their libels or even explain them. Their only defence was a series of motions to get the indicted editor cleared as not being responsible for what had appeared in the paper. Counsel labored over the contention that the accused was none of the things which the language of the law holds for libel. He was neither the "proprietor," "publisher," "editor," "printer," "author," nor a person "who uttered, gave, sold, or lent" a copy of the newspaper, but only the "manager." The employés gave testimony which would have been ludicrous but for the contempt it showed for court and community. The journalist who was the "managing editor" of the paper under the indicted chief editor was asked:

"Who was the head of the paper when you entered upon your duties as managing editor?"

"I do not know."

"Who hired you as managing editor?"

"I really can't say that I was hired at all."

"Who employed you to come to Toledo?" The witness had been an employé in Pennsylvania of the editor on trial, and had followed the latter to Toledo to take the place of managing editor.

"Nobody employed me."

The son of the indicted editor had also followed his father to Toledo, and was employed on his paper. Asked for what purpose he came, he said: "I had no purpose in coming."

The gentleman who had charge of the counting-room was asked who fixed his salary.

"I regulate my own."

The advertising manager declared:

"I have no knowledge who is my superior."

The accused had to let the case go to the jury without a spark of proof of the accusations which had filled the paper every day for months. He had no evidence to offer either that the charges were true, or that he believed them to be true. He stood self-confessed as having for years printed daily gross libels on citizens, officials, and community, as part of the tactics of a few outside men to prevent a free city from doing with its own means in its own affairs that which an overwhelming public opinion, and the legislative, executive, and judicial authorities, and its present antagonists themselves, had all sustained its right to do. The agent of this wrong was found guilty, and sentenced to imprisonment in the county jail, with heavy costs and fine. But sentence was suspended pending hearing of the motion for a new trial. This did not come up for a year. The court could find no error in the proceedings of the trial court, and could not sustain any of the objections made. But it found a point which even the lawyers had not hit on, and strained this far enough to grant the new trial. Then the convicted editor went before another judge—not the one who had tried him—pleaded guilty, and was fined, and so saved from jail.

XXIV

High Finance

Time ran on until the day was at hand for opening bids for the bonds. That was to be Wednesday. Then the counsel for the opposition notified the city that on Monday they would begin the taking of depositions. This was not then or afterwards done, but on the strength of the notification news despatches were sent over the country that the proceedings against the legality of the Toledo bonds were being "pressed." In consequence of this and other manoeuvres, when Wednesday came there were no bids. A hasty rally of some public-spirited capitalists at home, learning of the emergency, made up a subscription of $300,000. The names of the citizens who made this patriotic subscription were printed in the daily paper under the heading of "The Honor Roll."

Only by extraordinary manoeuvres could the market for such securities offered by such a community have been thus killed in a time of great general and local prosperity, and extraordinary they were.[1] What they were was formally and authoritatively ascertained by an investigation made by a committee appointed at a mass-meeting[2] of the citizens of Toledo called by the mayor, the Hon. J. K. Hamilton. The call ran:

> For the first time in the history of Toledo, its general bonds, secured by the faith and property of the city, and bearing a fair rate of interest, have been offered, and only such of them sold as were taken at home by popular subscription. It is deemed desirable that under such circumstances the citizens of Toledo should meet together and de-

[1] Lloyd neglects one point: there was considerable doubt about the adequacy of the city's sources of natural gas. [T.C.]

[2] October 19, 1889.

114

termine what further steps should be taken to carry out the will of
the peope as expressed by 62 per cent. of the voters of the city.
It is believed that with proper effort a large additional popular
subscription may be obtained, and thus notice given to the world that
notwithstanding all opposition the citizens of Toledo have confidence
in and will maintain the credit of this fair city, and that a great
enterprise undertaken by its people will not be defeated by the mach-
inations of private opposing interests, no matter how powerful and
unscrupulous.

The meeting appointed a committee of three—David Robinson,
Jr., Frank J. Scott, and Albert E. Macomber—"to prepare and cir-
culate throughout the financial circles of the country a pamphlet
which shall set forth the case of the city of Toledo in its struggle
against those who by anonymous circulars and other dishonorable
ways have attempted to prevent the sale of the Toledo natural-gas
bonds." This committee put the facts before the public in a very
able pamphlet, "The City of Toledo and Its Natural Gas Bonds."
In an official statement asked for by this committee the city natural-
gas trustees say: "Skilled writers were employed to furnish articles
for Eastern financial journals, to cast discredit on the bonds on the
very grounds that had been set aside by Judge Jackson's decision.
Not content with this open warfare, anonymous circulars were sent
to leading investment agencies in the United States, warning them
to beware of these bonds, as they were under the cloud of doubtful
constitutionality and an impending lawsuit. When the day arrived
for bidding for the bonds no bids were made. Agents of investors
were present, who came to bid, but by some unknown and powerful
influence they were induced not to put in their bids. The writers
are not aware that any similar mode of striking at the credit of a
whole community was ever before resorted to in this country. It is
an insult and a wrong not only to this city, against which it is
aimed, but to people of independence everywhere in the United
States who have a common interest in the maintenance of the
rights of all." [3]
Press despatches impugning the validity of the bonds and mis-
representing the facts were sent all over the country. The anonymous circulars referred to were mailed to all the leading banks,
investment agencies, capitalists, and newspapers. The New York
Mail and Express said: "It would be decidedly interesting to know
who is responsible for the . . . methods by which it was thought to

[3] City of Toledo and Its Natural Gas Bonds, pp. 6-7.

prevent the city from undertaking the enterprise. A number of volunteer attorneys and correspondents deluged bankers and newspapers with letters warning them against the bonds which the city proposes to issue, on the ground that it had no right to issue them. The *Mail and Express* received several communications of this kind."

The United States and state courts had refused on every ground to interfere with their issuance and sale. The invariable rule of the United States Supreme Court has been to treat as final and conclusive the decisions of the state courts as to state domestic issues. The only hope of the suit of "prominent taxpayers" was, therefore, that the Supreme Court of the United States would for their special profit reverse the practice to which it had consistently adhered since the establishment of the government.

They who had been so "anxious to get to the case as soon as possible" refrained from printing the record, a condition precedent to putting the case on the docket of the United States Supreme Court. The city wanted the decision, and in order that the case might not be dismissed for this failure to print the record, and a decision upon the merits be thus prevented, the city's gas trustees advanced the money—$1100—to the court printer for printing the record. Pushed thus against their will to trial, when the day came on which they must rise to state their case the opponents of Toledo folded their tents and stole silently away. On the motion of their attorney the case was dismissed, against the protest of the city. They paid all the costs, including the money advanced by the city for printing the record. To their defeat all along the line they did not want to add a formal decision against them from the Supreme Court, which was inevitable. And they ran away to fight another day.

Another purpose of these suits was confessed only a few weeks after this circular was issued. The existence of the suits was used to try to frighten the city's natural-gas trustees into accepting a "compromise." The compromise was that they should abandon the enterprise, sell out pipes and lands for a fraction of their worth, get their gas from the private company at higher rates, and put the city in its power for all time to come. "It will be three or four years before your case is through the Supreme Court," its representative told the natural-gas trustees, in urging them to accept. "You can't sell your bonds," he continued; "you have no money." The "compromise" was refused, but the city's pipe line had been delayed so

long that the profits of the company for another twelvemonth were
secure.

These litigations, the circulars, the press, were only part of the
campaign. One of the committees of the Common Council was
brought under control, and induced to throw technical difficulties
in the way of the sale of the bonds, which caused months of delay.[4]
Effort was made to get the Governor to appoint natural-gas trustees
hostile to the city, but failed. It was attempted, also without success, to get the Legislature to prevent the sale of the bonds at
private sale. During all this controversy the city was most fortunate
in receiving the needful authority from the State Legislature. This
was due mainly to a faithful and able representative of Toledo in
that body, the Hon. C. P. Griffin. He was offered every promise of
political preferment and other allurements to betray his constituents, but he always remained faithful. Without his support the
efforts of the city would have failed. His services amid great temptations deserve the grateful remembrance of the public.

Some of the devices of "private enterprise" were childish enough.
"A Business Men's Protest" was published, which proved under the
microscope to have been largely signed by men whose names could
not be found in the directory. A similarly formidable-looking remonstrance against the pipe-line bill was sent to the Legislature. It
had 1426 names; of these 464 could not be found in the directory,
and over 300 of the 962 remaining names signed the petition for the
city's bill. Many of them avowed that when they had signed the
"Remonstrance" it had a heading in favor of the pipe line, which
must have been changed afterwards. As part of the tactics of misin-
formation, a report was published—in January, 1890—claiming to
give the business of both the private companies; but the members of
the Council Committee on Gas, when afterwards examining the
books for the gas company, found that it gave the receipts of only
one company. A paper was prepared by a citizens' meeting for
circulation among the manufacturers to ascertain how much they
would contribute towards the city pipe line; but when reported
back to the meeting it had become, in some mysterious way, a paper
asking the manufacturers how much they would advance to quite a
different scheme, the effect of which would be to sell out the city
pipe line or convert it into a manufacturers' line.

These were the infantile methods of men who could not see the
ludicrousness of the position they put themselves in by such efforts

[4] Report of the Toledo Natural Gas Trustees, 1890, pp. 8-9.

to keep a business which they were constantly declaring to be hazardous and unprofitable.

Detectives appear in almost every scene of our story, and are as common in its plot as in any extravagant melodrama of the Bowery thirty years ago. To counteract the anonymous circulars the City Council sent a committee headed by Mayor Hamilton—the "war Mayor," one of the ablest lawyers of the city, upright and loyal at all times to Toledo—to visit the Eastern money-markets. The committee, in their official report, state that they were assured by responsible dealers in municipal securities in New York and Boston that they would bid for the entire amount to be sold. "We regret, however, to have to report that the powerful and influential parties who have on all occasions and in every way sought to obstruct and defeat the enterprise for which the proceeds of these bonds were to be used, in some way succeeded in inducing those who intended to purchase to withhold their bids—in fact, no matter how guarded our movements, we believe that every person or firm with whom we had interviews was reported to the agents of the Standard Oil Company, for in every instance where from our interviews we had encouragement that the bonds would be bid for, within a short time more or less influential agents of opponents interviewed these parties and succeeded in changing their minds."

The city was brought to the humiliation of seeing its officials meet in public session at an appointed hour to open bids it had invited from all the money centres for its bonds, only to have the news flashed all over the country that not a bid from abroad had been made. This opposition cost the city in one way and another not less than $1,000,000, according to the estimate of the city's natural-gas trustees. The feeling of the people was expressed in the following language in a circular sent out with the pamphlet report of the committee appointed in mass-meeting to make a statement of Toledo's case to the public:

"We have seen the modern aggregation of corporations—trusts— suppress other corporations in the same line of business. But this Toledo contest is believed to be the first instance where private corporations—creatures of the State—have assumed to exercise monarchical powers over a portion of the State—one of its leading municipalities; to dictate the policy of its people; to seek to control the legislation as to the laws that should be enacted for such portion of the State; to bribe and intimidate the votes of such city at the polls; to attempt to subsidize the press by the most liberal expenditure of money; to at last purchase, out and out, a heretofore leading paper of the city, place its own managers and attorneys as directors, import one of its long-trained men as editor, and turn this paper into an engine of attack upon the city, an attack upon the city's honor and credit, characterized by the most unscrupulous misrepresentation and a perfect abandonment of all the amenities of civilized warfare."

The Toledo public felt no doubt as to who were attacking it under the convenient anonymity of the two gas corporations. At a public conference, January 16, 1889, between the presidents of the private natural-gas companies and the people assembled in mass-meeting, the representatives of the former said the only condition on which the members of the oil trust had been induced to interest themselves in natural gas in Northwestern Ohio was that of absolute and unqualified control of the entire business through a majority of the stock of all the gas companies to be organized.

"The trust is interested in companies engaged in supplying natural gas?" the president of the oil trust was asked by the New York Legislature about this time.

"To a limited extent, yes."

"Have they a majority interest in any of these companies?"

"I think they have." [5]

When the warfare against Toledo became a scandal ringing throughout the country and beyond, the organ of the trust in Toledo attempted to make it appear that the oil trust was not the party in interest. But there was open confession on the record. Its connection and its control were admitted by two representatives in conference with a committee appointed by the mayor at their request to discuss the situation.[6] They described the circumstances under which the members of the oil trust had gone into the project of the Toledo line and the project of the natural-gas business. One of the two stated that he came into it as its "more direct representative." The pipe line of the private gas company was built, he went on to say, by one of the principal corporations in the oil trust. At the same interview it was admitted that the oil trust owned 60 per cent. of the natural-gas company's stock.

The people of Toledo did not surrender to this success of their enemies in the money-market. The bonds which calumny and espionage prevented them from selling at wholesale to the great

[5] Testimony, Trusts, New York Senate, 1888, p. 428.
[6] Toledo *Blade*, February 7 and 27, 1889.

capitalists of New York and Boston they took themselves at retail. The Legislature having given authority for such sales, a committee of one hundred had been appointed by the citizens' meeting, October 19, 1889, to canvass all the wards of the city for subscriptions to the gas bonds. "Gas Bond Pledges" were circulated, to which people subscribed according to their ability, in amounts ranging from $2 to $5000. The employes at the Wabash Railway's car shops sent in a list signed by fifty names for a total of $1102, an average of $22 each. The labor of two hundred men for a week without pay was offered the gas trustees as an earnest of the goodwill of the people. Piece by piece the city's pipe line was pushed through. At a critical moment a shrewd and patriotic contractor saved the enterprise by building a large part of the line, and taking for his pay the bonds the banks would not take. In June, 1890, the public were gratified by the announcement that their trustees had secured the means "for the construction of three miles more," making eight miles in all, or nearly one-fourth the entire line. In August a contract was made for five miles more, and so the work went on, step after step.

XXV

A Sunday in June

In the midst of the anxious discussion by the citizens of Toledo as to the character of the power which ruled them both by night and by day, the same question arose in the metropolitan religious press, but in its broader ethical aspects. After the petition of Toledo to be allowed to take the control of its light, heat, and power into its own hands had been laid before the Legislature, the *National Baptist* of Philadelphia, in an article on the trusts, criticised them as the prophet Nathan would have done. It gave to that in oil, "of course, the bad pre-eminence in all this matter." "This corporation has, by ability, by boldness, by utter unscrupulousness, by the use of vast capital, managed to control every producer, every carrier, to say nothing of the legislatures and courts." The *Examiner*, the leading religious weekly of the Baptist denomination in New York, rose against this. "We can readily understand how there should be differences of opinion in the matter of these trusts, and their influence is a proper subject of discussion; but to make it the occasion of so unjust and intemperate an attack on Christian men of the highest excellence of character is something that was not expected from a paper bearing such a name. The four most prominent men in the oil trust are eminent Baptists, who honor their religious obligations, and contribute without stint to the noblest Christian and philanthropic objects. . . . All of them illustrate in their daily lives their reverence for living Christianity."

The *National Baptist* did not submit to this attempt to cite men's creeds to prevent judgment on their deeds. It quoted the reply Macaulay makes Milton give to the similar pleas urged for King Charles: "For his private virtues they are beside the question. If he oppress and extort all day, shall he be held blameless because he prayeth a night and morning?" It held to its ground, and cited against the trust the recorded evidence, but it declared it was "a marked breach of propriety for the *Examiner* to bring their private character into the discussion." The *National Baptist,* going on to speak in praise of a series of lively cartoons in *Harper's Weekly* on the Forty Thieves of the Trusts and similar subjects, said, with some sadness: "It will be a sorry spectacle if the secular papers shall be ranged on the side of justice and the human race, while the defence of monopoly shall be left to the so-called representatives of the religious press."

Later, March 20, 1890, the *Examiner* returned again to its discussion of the religious performances of the chiefs of the oil trust as a matter of public importance. Of one of them it said: "The prayer-meetings of the Fifth Avenue Church are on Wednesday evening, and no business man in the church is less likely to be absent from one of them than he. His wife and children, when they are in the city, come with him, and it is by no means an unusual thing for the whole family to take part, each of them occupying one or two minutes of time. He and they are at church every Sunday when in the city, and no husband and wife keep up the good old Baptist habit more faithfully of exchanging a kind word with the brethren and sisters after the regular services are over. He dresses plainly, and so do his family, and every one of them has a kind heart and a pleasant word for all. They are among the last to leave the church and the prayer-meeting. Now the question is, How is it, as things go, that a man possessing the great wealth imputed to him should have so warm a fraternity of feeling for the lowly in their temporal conditions? And is there not an example here that might well be imitated in all the churches of our Lord?"

"They are worth a bit of careful study," says another paper of the trustees, "and no place is quite so convenient as when they are at church. Their interest in religion is as sincere as their belief in oil. From the moment they enter church until they leave they are examples that Christians of high and low degree might follow with profit." "They have made the most of both worlds," writes another journalist. The oil trust was criticized by the Rev. Washington Gladden at Chautauqua, in 1889. One of its prominent officials, as reported in a friendly journal, defended it as "a sound Christian institution; and all these communistic attacks are due entirely to the jealousy of those who cannot stand other people's prosperity." [1]

"In Anniversary week," in Boston, in May, 1889, at the meeting of the American Baptist Education Society, the secretary said he had an announcement to make. "It had been whispered about," says the New York *Examiner* of May 23, 1889, from whose friendly account we are quoting, "that something important was to occur at this meeting, and a breathless silence awaited the announcement. Holding up a letter, the secretary said that he had here a pledge from a princely giver to our educational causes, naming him (here he was interrupted by a tremendous cheer), of $600,000 for the proposed Chicago college. . . . This statement was followed by a perfect bedlam of applause, shouts, and waving of handkerchiefs. One brother on the platform was so excited that he flung his hat up into the air, and lost it among the audience." Eloquent speeches at once overflowed the lips of the leading men of the meeting, which was a delegate assembly. They sprang to their feet, one after the other, and mutually surpassed each other in praising God and the giver of this gift, which was equal to his income for a fortnight. "I scarcely dare trust myself to speak," said a doctor of divinity. "The coming to the front of such a princely giver—the man to lead. . . . It is the Lord's doing. . . . As an American, a Baptist, and a Christian I rejoice in this consummation. God has kept Chicago for us; I wonder at his patience." Another reverend doctor said: "The Lord hath done great things for us. . . . The man who has given this money is a godly man, who does God's will as far as he can find out what God's will is."

The Sunday following a special service was held in the churches throughout the country in behalf of further help in "the new educational crisis." Many eulogistic sermons were preached that day by the leading clergymen of the denomination. "And so," one of them is reported to have said, "when a crisis came God had a man ready to meet it. . . . An institution was bound to come, and unless a God-fearing man established it it was likely to be materialistic, agnostic. . . . In this emergency, and in God's providence, society raised up a man with a colossal fortune, and a heart as large as his fortune." "God," said the Chicago *Standard*, a religious weekly, "has guided us and provided us a leader and a giver, and so brought us out into a large place."

The next year after the Boston meeting the Church celebrated its

"Anniversary week" in the city which was to be the seat of the new college. And the anniversary closed with a jubilee meeting, which filled the largest assembly room in America. "All the church-going people of Chicago must have attended," one of the daily papers said. It was addressed by the principal clergymen of the denomination from all parts of the country. Again, as at Boston, the centre of interest was the gift of a fortnight's income to the university. A telegram making the gift conclusive, since the conditions on which it was promised had been complied with, was read. Cheer after cheer rose from the assembly, and oratory and music expressed the emotion of the audience. The divine who made the closing speech declared that he needed ice on his head on account of the joyful excitement of the occasion. The cheers and the handclapping closed again, as at Boston, with the spirited singing of the Doxology. Not only in the religious press of all denominations, but in the worldly press, the topic was the best of "copy." The great dailies gave columns, and even pages to the incident, and to the subsequent gift from the same source of larger sums. "Conspicuously providential," "princely," "grand," "munificent contribution," "man of God," were the phrases of praise. A writer in the New York *Independent* said: "Your correspondent speaks from opportunities of personal observation in saying that pecuniary benefaction to a public cause seldom if ever, in his belief, flowed from a purer Christian source." The only recorded note of dissent came from a humbler source. Under the text, "I hate robbery as a burnt-offering," a weekly business journal said: "The endowment of an educational institution where the studies shall be limited to a single course, and that a primary course in commercial integrity, would be a still more advantageous outlet for superabundant capital. Such an institution would fill a crying want."

XXVI

Toledo Victor

It was remarkable to see the revival of the passion of freedom of 1776 and 1861 in the editorials, speeches, resolutions of public meetings, and the talk of the common people in Toledo as in Columbus. The example of "the heroic liberty-loving people of Boston" was held up in every aspect to fire the heart of Toledo not to be frightened into subjection to the foreign power that threatened them. To resist "the domination of an economic monarchy" was the appeal made in posters with which the town was placarded.

"During all the time George III.'s soldiers were quartered in Boston that monarch did not spend as much money to bring the city to terms as has been spent in this effort to subjugate the city of Toledo," said Alderman Macomber.

"A people like those of Toledo," said one of them in the press, "when once united and determined as they now are, cannot be subjugated by any combination of mercenaries yet known."

"It is evident," the Toledo *Sunday Journal* said, "that the people of Toledo have come ʻo a full realization of the truth that the money saved by the independent pipe line, though great, is a matter of little importance compared with the social and political issues involved. It would be a thousand times better," it continued, "to utterly bankrupt the city than permit the oil combination to win. The fight was not for the present alone, but it was for the present and future, and for all time to come. It was not for the people of Toledo alone, but it was for the whole Union, though God had chosen the people of Toledo for the struggle."

The most serious crisis in the contest was still to come. In 1892 the gas wells of the city began to do what the people of the city will never do—surrender to the enemy. When the oil trust found, after years of opposition in the Legislature, the courts, and the gas-fields, that it had been helpless to prevent Toledo from getting ample tracts of excellent gas territory, with some of the largest gas wells in the field, and equal to the supply of the entire consumption, domestic and manufacturing, it turned to other tactics.

All about this territory secured by Toledo and found so productive the private companies of the trust proceeded to buy or lease and to sink wells. The trust shut off all its own wells, except those adjacent to the city territory, and for two years drew exclusively from the wells nearest those of the city. When the city's line was completed to the wells the volume of gas was found to be largely reduced. It had been drawn off into the wells of the opposition. In the spring of 1892 the private companies resolved to put in pumps to strengthen the diminished natural pressure, but to prevent the city from doing the same thing. Then, with their pumps alone at work, the pressure could be so much further reduced as to render the Toledo pipe line valueless. To this end all efforts were directed. The newspapers were kept full of matter showing how impossible it was to pump gas, that all the money expended in pumps would be just so much wasted, and that the companies had canvassed the matter fully, but abandoned the idea. Column after column of inspired interviews filled the papers, all admonishing the city of Toledo not to commit such an act of folly as to put in gas pumps. Then application was made to enjoin the sale of the bonds authorized by the council and the Legislature for pumps. So month after month dragged along. The bonds remained unsold, and the pumps unobtainable.

The injunction was refused both by the Court of Common Pleas and by the Circuit Court. But there was a right of appeal to the Ohio Supreme Court until the beginning of 1892. Boston bankers had subscribed for a large block of the bonds, but withdrew upon learning these facts. "It is possible for the contestants," the lawyers advised them, "to carry the matter to the Supreme Court. This, we understand, they propose to do." The simple assertion of a purpose to continue the litigation was enough to defeat the sale of the bonds. The payment of costs and lawyers' fees would be a very moderate price to pay for compelling the city's gas plant to go past mid-winter without the pumps indispensable for its operation. One of the employees of the private pipe line, according to an account in one of the Toledo papers, declared to a reporter that "if we could not prevent the city from putting in a [pumping] plant any other way, we would blow it up with dynamite." [1]

The city attempted to use its income from the sales of gas to buy pumps. An injunction was applied for and granted. This emergency was finally met by having the gas trustees hand over to the city authorities the accumulated earnings they were forbidden by the court to spend themselves. The city thereupon turned around and invested this money in the gas bonds. In this way the identical money the gas trustees could not use while it remained in their hands was made available to them by passing through the hands of the Sinking Fund Trustees, and coming back to them. Thus the natural-gas trustees were enabled to make a contract in September, 1892, for pumps to assist the flow of gas to the city.

The gas pumps are a patented device. The private companies, wanting all the profit of everything, had had their pumps made at their own factory. The city made its contract directly with the owner of the patents. The result was that the city got its pumps in place in time to save the city pipe line, while its opponents were delayed by the inexperience of their own pump-makers. This was the most critical period in our history. Greed had again defeated itself. Had the opposition gone to the owner of the patents he would have been unable afterwards to take the city's contract and complete it in time, and the effort to make the city line valueless would have succeeded—for the time being, at least. The bonds in question were afterwards held valid by the Supreme Court.

Private enterprise cannot find rhetoric strong enough to express its contempt for the inefficiency, costliness, and despotisms of public enterprise. Private enterprise put at $6,000,000—twelve times the amount of the property they reported for taxation—the "capital" stock invested by the two natural-gas companies. The city pipe line was capitalized (bonded) at just what it cost—a little more than a million. The city trustees built a better pipe line than private enterprise had laid. The private line was of cheap iron of 14-feet lengths, while Toledo's was in 24-feet pieces. One of the private lines was laid with rubber joints and in shallow trenches, in many places of not more than plough depth. It leaked at almost every joint; its course could be traced across the fields by the smell of gas and the blighted line of vegetation. There were frequent explosions from the escaping gas; lives and property were much endangered. The city line was laid with lead joints, and had every device that

[1] See ch. xxxi.

engineering experience could suggest for its success, and was so constructed that it could be cleaned or repaired, and freed from liquids interfering with the flow of gas, without shutting off the supply—features the other pipe had not. The action of the city trustees had to endure the microscopic scrutiny of friend and foe. No one was able to show as to a single acre that the title was defective, or that it could have been bought for less, or to find any taint of a job in the construction of the pipe. A committee of the city council sat and probed for six weeks, but failed to find any evidence whatever to confirm the reported "irregularities."

April 8, 1893, the natural-gas trustees of Toledo had the happiness of being able to give formal notice to the city auditor that no taxes need be levied to pay the interest on the gas bonds, as it "can easily be met from the revenues derived from the sale of natural gas." The city pipe line was on a paying basis at last. Toledo had vindicated its claim to be a free city. The completion of the enterprise had been delayed three years. A loss of not less than two million dollars had been laid on the city, but its victory was worth many times that. Toledo's victory showed the country, in full and successful detail, a plan of campaign. It was not a local affair, but one of even more than national importance, for the oil combination has invaded four continents. This struggle and its results of good omen will pass into duly recorded history as a warning and an encouragement to people everywhere who wish to lead the life of the commonwealth.

XXVII

"You Are A—Senator"

Representative Hopkins, of Pennsylvania, rose in his place in the House of Representatives on May 16, 1876, and asked unanimous consent to offer a resolution for the appointment of a committee of five to investigate the charges that "many industries are crippled and threatened with extreme prostration" by the discrimination of the railroads, and to report a bill for the regulation of interstate commerce. This was the first move to reopen in Congress the great question, first on the order of the day both in England and in America, which had been smothered by the Committee of Commerce of 1872. It required unanimous consent to bring the resolution before the House.

"Instantly," said Representative Hopkins, in describing the occurrence afterwards,[1] "I heard the fatal words 'I object.' The objector was Mr. Henry B. Payne, of Cleveland." Other members appealed to Mr. Payne to withdraw his objection.

The Speaker of the House: "Does the gentleman from Ohio withdraw his objection?"

Mr. Payne: "I do not."

In a private conference which followed between Representative Payne and Representative Hopkins, the former said, as Mr. Hopkins relates: "What he objected to in my resolution was the creation of a special committee; but if I would again offer it and ask that it be referred to the Committee of Commerce he would not object. I thought perhaps there was something reasonable in his objection. A special committee would probably require a clerk, which would be an expense. He looked to me so like a frugal Democrat, who had

[1] New York *Herald*, January 19, 1884.

great confidence in the regular order of established committees and
did not want the country to be taxed for clerks attending to the
business of special committees—I say that he so impressed me that,
as the record will show, I adopted his suggestion."

When the Committee of Commerce to which the investigation
was accordingly referred began its investigation, a member of the
oil combination, not then, as later, a member of the Senate, took his
seat by the ear of the chairman, who was from his State, "presiding,"
as the oil producers said in a public appeal, "behind the seat of the
chairman." [2] The financial officer of the oil combination was called
as a witness, but refused to answer the questions of the committee as
to the operations of the company or its relations with the railroads.
The vice-president of the Pennsylvania Railroad also refused to
answer questions. On the plea of needing time to decide how to
compel these witnesses to answer, the committee let the railroad
vice-president go until he should be recalled. But the committee
never decided, and the witnesses were never recalled. The committee
never reported to Congress, made no complaint of the contempt of
its witnesses, and the investigation of 1876, like that of 1872, came
to a mute and inglorious end.

When Representative Hopkins applied to the clerk of the committee for the testimony, he was told, to his amazement, that it
could not be found. "Judge Reagan," he relates,[3] "who was a stanch
friend of the bill"—for the regulation of the railroads—"and very
earnest for the investigation, and who at the time was a member of
the committee, told me that it had been stolen."

Eight years after "I object" the people of Ohio were a suppliant
before the Senate of the United States. They believed that their
dearest rights had been violated, and they prayed for redress to the
only body which had power to give it. Officially by the voice of both
Houses of the State Legislature and the governor, unofficially by the
press, by the public appeals of leading men, by the petitions of
citizens, press, leaders, and people, regardless of party, the commonwealth asserted that the greatest wrong possible in a republic had
been done their members, and sued for restitution. They declared it
to be their belief that against their will, as the result of violation of
the laws, a man had taken their seat in the Senate of the United
States who was not their senator, that they had been denied repre-

[2] Appeal to the Executive of Pennsylvania by the Petroleum Producers' Union,
1878, Trusts, Congress, 1888, p. 354.
[3] New York *Herald*, January 19, 1884.

sentation by the senator of their choice; and they demanded that, in accordance with immemorial usage, the evidence they had to offer should be examined, and their right of representation in the Senate of the United States restored to them, if it should be found to have been taken from them. After the Legislature had examined sixty-four witnesses, the Ohio House of Representatives resolved that "ample testimony was adduced to warrant the belief that . . . the seat of Henry B. Payne in the United States Senate was purchased by the corrupt use of money." The Ohio Senate charged that "the election of Henry B. Payne as Senator of the United States from Ohio . . . was procured and brought about by the corrupt use of money, . . . and by other corrupt means and practices."

Both Houses passed with these resolutions an urgent request for investigation by the Senate of the United States.[4]

Mr. Payne's election by the Legislature was a thunder-clap to the people of Ohio. They did not know he was a candidate. Who was to be United States Senator was of course one of the issues in the election of the Ohio Legislature of 1884, and the Democratic voters who elected the majority of that Legislature had sent them to the State Capitol to make George H. Pendleton or Durbin Ward senator. One of the leading newspaper men of the State testified: "I went over the entire State during the campaign. . . . Out of the eighty-eight counties I attended fifty-four Democratic conventions and wrote them up, giving the sentiment of the people as nearly as I could, and during that entire canvass I never heard a candidate for the Legislature say that he was for Henry B. Payne for United States Senator; but every man I ever talked with was either for George H. Pendleton or General Ward. I think out of the Democratic candidates throughout the State I conversed with at least two-thirds of them."[5] As was afterwards stated before the Senate of the United States by the representatives of the people of Ohio, "He was in no wise publicly connected with the canvass for the Senate, nor had the most active, honorable, and best-posted politicians in the State heard his name in connection with the senatorial office until subsequent to the October election [of the Legislature]. He was absolutely without following."[6]

[4] Report No. 1490, United States Senate, 49th Congress, 1886, p. 1.
[5] Testimony, Appendix to the Journal of the House of Representatives of the State of Ohio, 67th General Assembly, 1886, vol. lxxxii., p. 499.
[6] Report No. 1490, United States Senate, 49th Congress, 1886, p. 60.

The press, without regard to party, gave voice to the popular wrath. Scores of the Democratic newspapers of Ohio went into mourning. One of them said: "The whole Democratic Legislature was made rotten by the money that was used to buy and sell the members like so many sheep." Many representative Democrats of the State privately and publicly declared their belief in the charges of corruption. Allen G. Thurman, who had been a senator and representative at Washington, said: "There is something that shocks me in the idea of crushing men like Pendleton and Ward, who have devoted the best portion of their lives to the maintenance of Democracy, by a combination against them of personal hatred and overgrown wealth. . . . I want to see all the Democrats have a fair chance according to their merits, and do not want to see a political cutthroat bossism inaugurated for the benefit of a close party corporation or syndicate." Again he said: "Syndicates purchase the people's agents, and honest men stand aghast." [7]

It was the "irony of fate" that this Legislature, like the 44th Congress, had been specially elected to represent opposition to monopolies. Of course the Legislature that had done this thing was not to be persuaded, bullied, or shamed into any step towards exposure or reparation. But the people, usually so forgetful, nursed their wrath. They made the scandal the issue of the next State election, and put the Legislature into other hands. The new Legislature then forwarded formal charges to the Senate of the United States, and a demand for an investigation. The State of Ohio made its solemn accusation and prayer for an investigation through all the organs of utterance it had: the press of both parties; honored men, both Republican and Democratic; both Houses of the State Legislature and its senator whose seat was unchallenged—an aggregate representing a vast majority of the people of the State. The Hon. John Little and the Hon. Benjamin Butterworth, former Attorney-General of Ohio, both members of Congress, had been delegated to present the case of the State. They made formal charges, based on evidence given under oath or communicated in writing by reputable citizens, who were willing to testify under oath. None of the matter was presented on mere hearsay or rumor.[8] No charge was made to connect Senator Payne personally with the corruption. His denials and those of his friends of any participation by him were therefore mere evasions of the actual charge—that his election had

[7] Report No. 1490, United States Senate, 49th Congress, 1886, pp. 77, 78.
[8] *Ibid.*, p. 58.

been corruptly procured for him, not by him. The substance of their accusation, as contained in their statement and the papers forwarded by the Legislature, was as follows:[9]

That among the chief managers of Mr. Payne's canvass, and those who controlled its financial operations, were four of the principal members in Ohio of the oil trust; its treasurer, the vice-president of one of its most important subordinate companies, its Cincinnati representative, and another—all of whom were named.

That one of these four, naming him, who was given the financial management of the Payne campaign at Columbus, carried $65,000 with him, "next to his skin," to Columbus to use in the election, as he had stated to an intimate friend whose name would be given.

That the cashier of the bank in Cleveland, where the treasurer of the oil combination kept one of his bank accounts, would testify that this money was procured on a check given by this treasurer of the oil trust to another of its officials, and passed over by him to its Cincinnati agent, who drew out the cash.

That the back room used by the Payne manager at Columbus as his office displayed such large amounts of money in plain view that it looked like a bank, and that the employé who acted there as his clerk stated upon his return home that he had never seen so much money handled together in his life.

That a prominent gentleman, going to the room used by the Payne managers for a "converter," had said that he saw "canvas bags and coin bags and cases for greenbacks littered and scattered around the room and on the table and on the floor . . . with something green sticking out," which he found to be money.

That members who had been earnest supporters of Pendleton were taken one by one by certain guides to this room which looked like a bank, and came out with an intense and suddenly developed dislike of civil-service reform (Mr. Pendleton's measure), and proceeded to vote for Mr. Payne; and that these conversions were uniformly attended with thrift, sudden, extensive, and so irreconcilable with their known means of making money as to be a matter of remark among their neighbors; and that "the reasons for the change (of vote) were kept mainly in this room, passed by delivery, and could be used to buy real estate."

That this use of money in large amounts to procure the sudden

[9] Report No. 1490, United States Senate, 49th Congress, 1886, pp. 37, 40, 66; Miscellaneous Document No. 106, United States Senate, 49th Congress, 1886, pp. 32, 46, 214, and *passim*.

conversions of Pendleton legislators to Payne would be shown by numerous witnesses, generally Democrats, several of them lawyers of great distinction and high ability.

That the editor and proprietor of the principal Democratic journal in Ohio had stated, as was sworn to, that he had spent $100,000 to elect Payne, and that it cost a great deal of money to get those representatives and senators to vote for Payne, and they had to be bought. "It took money, and a good deal of it, to satisfy them," and he complained that the oil trust had not reciprocated in kind. This statement was made by one of his editorial writers, who after making it was discharged. The latter subsequently put it into the form of an affidavit.

That Senator Pendleton would testify that more than enough of the legislators to give him the election had been pledged to him.

That a member of the Legislature, a State senator, had himself stated that he had received $5000 to vote for Payne,[10] and had offered the same amount to an associate if he would do the same; and that after the election this member opened a new bank account, depositing $2500 in his wife's name, who immediately transferred it to him.

The State Legislature could not compel the witnesses to testify. Only the United States Senate could do this, and it was deterred from doing so by this concealment of the fact that the investigation, instead of failing because of no basis, had struck firmer ground. The proffer of evidence was of such a character that, as has been well said, none of the lawyers of the Senate committee who voted against recommending investigation "would have failed to recommend thorough investigation of such an incident if it had been relevant to an alleged title set up against a private client." [11] But the Senate Committee on Privileges and Elections—Senators Pugh, Saulsbury, Vance, and Eustis voting against Hoar and Frye—recommended the Senate not to investigate, and the Senate adopted this report.

The debate upon the recommendation of the committee not to investigate was impassioned. Senator Hoar said: "The adoption of this majority report . . . will be the most unfortunate fact in the history of the Senate." When the vote of the Senate not to investigate was announced, Senator Edmunds turned to his neighbor in

[10] Report No. 1490, United States Senate, 49th Congress, 1886, p. 50.
[11] *The Payne Bribery Case and the United States Senate,* by Albert H. Walker.

the Senate and summed up the verdict of posterity in these words: "This is a day of infamy for the Senate of the United States."

The same Legislature which sent Senator Payne to the Senate defeated the bill to allow the Cleveland independent refiners to build a pipe line to furnish themselves with oil. The defeat of the bill was accomplished by a lobby whose work was so openly shameless that it was characterized by the Ohio press "as an indelible disgrace to the State." The bill was one of many attempts which have been made by the people of Ohio and Pennsylvania, without success, to get from their Legislature the right to build pipe lines. It has been tried to get laws to regulate the charges of the existing line, but without success. The history of the pipe-line bills in these legislatures for the past ten years has been a monotonous record of an unavailing struggle of a majority of millions to apply legal and constitutional restraints to a minority of a few dozens. The means employed in the Ohio Legislature of 1885 to defeat a bill giving equality in pipe-line transportation to refiners in competition with the oil trust, which owned the existing pipe lines, were of such a sort that that body has gone into the history of the State as the "Coal-oil Legislature." It is stated by Hudson, in his *Railways and the Republic,* that the Democratic agent of the bribery openly threatened to publish the list he had of the members of the Legislature he had purchased, and that in consequence of this threat proceedings which had been begun against him for outraging the House by appearing on the floor in a state of gross intoxication were abandoned.[12]

The use this senator made of his seat throws light where none is needed. Again, in 1887, the great question of 1876 of the control of the highways came up before Congress. The agitation of nearly twenty years had come to a point. Thirty of the States and Territories of the Union had established commissions or passed laws to regulate the railroads. Congress had before it the Interstate Commerce bill forbidding discriminations, and creating the Interstate Commerce Commission as a special tribunal to prevent and punish the crime. There had been investigation, debates, amendments, meetings of conference committees of both Houses. It was proposed to "recommit" the bill to prevent its passage for an indefinite time. Mr. Payne voted "Yes." Then the question before the Senate is,

[12] Hudson's *Railways and the Republic,* p. 467.

Shall the bill become a law? Senator Payne's name is called. He votes:

"No."

It is the same question as in 1876, and the same vote. Against the investigation, first and then the legislation, his word is:

"I object."

XXIX

"The Commodity Is Not So Good as Before"
——Lord Coke

Three hundred years ago Lord Coke, in the "Case of the Monopolies," [1] declared these to be the inevitable result of monopoly: the price of the commodity will be raised; the commodity is not so good as before; it tends to the impoverishment of artisans, artificers, and others.

In 1878 and 1879, when railway presidents were saying "No" to every application of the few remaining independents for passage along the road to market,[2] and the oil combination was supreme from the well to the lamp, a concerted protest was made against its oil by commercial bodies representing trade all over Europe. An international congress was held specially to consider means for the protection of the European consumer, by the interposition of the governments of Europe and America, or by commercial measures.

The superiority of its barrels was specially mentioned by the head of the oil combination to explain why all competitors failed. "All its advantages," he said in court in Cleveland, "are legitimate business advantages, due to the very large volume of supplies which it purchases, its long continuance in the business, the experience it has thereby acquired, the knowledge of all the avenues of trade, the skill of experienced employés, the possession and use of all the latest and most valuable mechanical improvements, appliances, and processes for the distillation of crude oil, and in the manufacture of its own barrels, glue, etc., by reason of which it is enabled to put the oil on the market at a cost of manufacture much less

[1] II. Coke, 84.
[2] See ch. viii.

than by others not having equal advantages." But the Bremen congress made a special attack on the "barrels" and "glue." It complained that "the continental petroleum trade has suffered heavy losses on account of inferior barrels," and demanded that the oil combination should "only use barrels of well-seasoned, air-dried, split (not sawed) white oak staves and heads." It even particularized that the barrels should be "painted with blue linseed-oil paint, and supplied with double, strong head-hoops," and "more carefully glued, and not filled until the glue is thoroughly dry."

"They were substantially without competition," was said in explanation of the poor quality of the product sent to Europe, and also "to all parts of this country. The quality of the oil which they sent was not a matter of first-class importance for them to retain their business." It was "a negligence which came in a great measure from the absence of competition." This witness was asked by the lawyer of the combination if he meant the committee to understand that it "was committing suicide by furnishing a continuously deteriorating article of oil to the consumer."

"They were not committing suicide, because they had the business in their own hands almost exclusively at that time." [3]

This was in 1879, and the complaints of the quality of American oil sent abroad continue to this day. Export oil, the Interstate Commerce Commission say, in 1892, "is an inferior oil." [4]

By one of those coincidences in which the world of cause and effect abounds, the Fire Marshal of Boston, in the same year in which Joshua Merrill described his fruitless efforts to continue the manufacture of a first-class oil,[5] found it necessary to warn the people against the dangerous stuff they were burning in their lamps. In his report in 1888 he called attention to the fact that one-tenth, nearly, of all the fires in Boston the preceding year had been caused by the explosion of kerosene or by its accidental combustion. He got samples of the oil used in a number of the places where fires had occurred from explosion, and had them analyzed by professors of the Institute of Technology in Boston and of the School of Mines of Columbia College in New York. They found them to be below the quality required by the State. Singularly enough, one of the State oil inspectors, examining similar samples, declared them to

[3] Testimony, New York Assembly "Hepburn" Report, pp. 3683-94.
[4] Titusville and Oil City Independents' cases, Interstate Commerce Commission Reports, vol. v, p. 415.
[5] See pp. 74-75.

be above the standard of the State. The Boston *Herald*, discussing the matter, pointed out that the oil inspectors were paid by the owner of the oil. This, it said, placed inspectors practically under the oil combination, which has ways, it continued, of making things unpleasant for inspectors who make reports unsatisfactory to it. The fire marshal's conclusion in all the cases he investigated of these fires by explosion was: "I have felt warranted in every instance in attributing the blame to the inferior quality of kerosene used." [6]

An investigation was made of the conduct of the State oil inspector by the Committee on Illuminating Oils of the Minnesota Senate, in 1891. The committee say in their report, which was adopted by the Senate:

"The testimony further shows that stencils were left with different oil companies by the State inspector or his deputy, by which the companies caused their barrels containing oil to be branded by their own employés, without the supervision of any State official. It appears that after the arrangement for the payment of the inspectors' and deputies' salaries by the oil companies was made, the attitude of the inspector towards his duties may be summed up in a few words of his testimony: 'I am under no obligation to the State of Minnesota. The Standard Oil Company paid me.' " [7]

Some power, certainly not originating among the people, has for years, in States where the inspection laws required a high quality of oil, been at work procuring a reduction of the test. In some cases this has been accomplished only after persistent lobbying for years, as in Michigan. The test in Michigan has been lowered by legislation, as in Nebraska, and with similar results. The reports of the Michigan State Board of Health show that as the standard was lowered, fires and deaths from explosions increased. The Detroit *Tribune* of December 27, 1891, says that the reduction of the test in Michigan and Nebraska is due to the avarice of the producers (refiners) and nothing less than criminal carelessness of the legislators. The dangerous constituents of petroleum, such as naphtha and gasolene, are indistinguishable by the eye of the buyer from kerosene. They can be as easily mixed with it as hot and warm water with cold. The reductions of the test in various States permit mixtures more hazardous than dynamite to be sold to the people, lulled into reliance upon the State inspectors. "The advantage to the oil company," says the Detroit

[6] Second Annual Report, Fire Marshal of Boston, May, 1888, p. 9.
[7] Journal of the Senate of Minnesota, March 1891, p. 716.

(Michigan) *Times* of April 30, 1891, "is obvious. Naphtha and gasolene are worth, perhaps, three cents a gallon. Kerosene is worth three times as much. A test which allows one quart of kerosene and three quarts of gasolene to constitute a gallon of merchantable illuminating oil will enable a few more colleges to be endowed, though increasing the death-roll in a notable degree."

XXX

"To Get All We Can"

Are the combinations, trusts, syndicates of modern industry organized scarcity or organized plenty? Dearness or cheapness? "They are doing their work cheaper," said one of the oil combination of himself and his associates, "than any rival organization can afford to do it, and that is their policy, and by that only will they survive." [1]

"We think our American petroleum is a very cheap light. It is our pleasure to try to make it so," said its head.[2]

"Our object has always been to reduce rates, and cheapen the product, and increase its consumption by making the lowest price possible to the consumer," said another.[3]

Even if this were true—But is it true?

The purchase of the refineries at Baltimore by the oil combination in 1877, under the name of the Baltimore United Oil Company, was immediately followed by an advance in price. The Baltimore *Sun*, in December, 1877, said: "The combination has already begun to exert its influence on the market. Oil for home consumption was yesterday quoted at 14 cents, having raised from 11½ cents, the quotation on Wednesday. The combination will not make contracts ahead, which might be interpreted to mean an intended advance in price." In Buffalo the manager of one of the properties of the oil combination said in evidence: "My son is on a committee, he told me, that regulates the price of oil." [4] While the trust

---

[1] Testimony, Corners, New York Senate, 1883, p. 670.
[2] Testimony, Trusts, Congress, 1888, p. 389.
[3] *Ibid.*, p. 317.
[4] Buffalo Lubricating Oil Company *vs.* Everest *et al.* Supreme Court Erie Co., N.Y., 1886.

had the trade of Buffalo to itself, it held the price of oil at a high rate. "In Buffalo there were then no rival works," said State's Attorney Quinby to the jury who were trying its representatives for conspiracy against a competing refinery, "and we were paying for kerosene 18 cents a gallon. To-day, with the little Buffalo company in the market making kerosene, you can get it for 6 cents a gallon."

This Buffalo competitor was a very modest affair, insignificant in capital and resources, but it cut down the price of oil as far away as Boston. It established there an agent who "went around" and "cut the prices down," and then the agent of the combination "went around and cut the prices further," as its Boston employé described it. He was instructed, he said, "to follow them down, . . . only not to sell at a loss." Before this competitor came he had been selling oil as high as 20 cents a gallon. "We got the price down to 18 cents, and got down then, I believe, to 8 cents, so that I have been selling them since then at 8 cents." [5] Eight cents, then, was not at a loss—since he had been told "not to sell at a loss"—and yet these passionate pilgrims of cheapness had been making the Boston buyer pay 20 cents! "I have been selling since at 8 cents," he says. This testimony was given in 1886; the reduction to 8 cents from 20 was made in 1882. Four years' consumption of this oil had been given to the buyer in Boston at 8 cents a gallon instead of 20, in consequence of the entrance of so insignificant a competitor.

The committee of Congress which investigated trusts in 1889 gathered a great deal of sworn evidence—the details of which remained uncontradicted, and which were met only by general statements like those quoted at the head of this chapter—showing how extortionate prices had been charged until competition appeared, that in all cases a war of extermination had been made upon those competitors, and that when their business was destroyed prices were put up again. Losses in competitive wars were merely investments from which to draw dividends in perpetuity. The "cheapness" of the combination followed the cheapness of competitors, and was merely a feint, one of the approaches in a siege to overcome the inner citadel of cheapness, a strategic cheapness to-day on which to build dearness forever. This battle of prices is shown in a table covering fifty towns in Texas, Mississippi, Louisiana, Alabama, Tennessee, Georgia, Kentucky, for three to five years. The appear-

[5] Testimony, Trusts, Congress, 1888, pp. 846-47.

ance of competitive oil, for instance, cut the prices of oil from 15 cents a gallon down to 10 in Paris, Texas; from 25 to 15 in Calvert, Texas; from 22 cents to 10 in Austin, Texas; from 16 to 5 in Little Rock, Arkansas—evidently a war price; from 16 to 8½ in Huntsville, Alabama; from 16 to 8 in Memphis, Tennessee, and so on.[6] The committee of Congress submit pages of evidence of reimposition of high prices the moment competition was killed off. If the combination found a rival dealer out of oil for only a day it "popped the prices up 3½ cents."[7] "One day," wrote one of the dealers, "oil is up to 20 cents and over, and when any person attempts to import here, other than the vassals 'of the oil combination,' it is put down to 7 cents a gallon."[8]

The trust, notwithstanding its powers of "producing the very best oil at the lowest possible price," compels dealers to sign away their rights to buy oil where they can buy it the cheapest or best. When opposition is encountered from any of the retailers in a town the plan of campaign of its "war" is very simple. Some one is found who is willing for hire to sell his oils at a cut price until the rest are made sick enough to surrender. Then contracts are made with all the dealers, binding them to buy of no one else, and prices are put up to a point at which a handsome profit is assured. After this competitors can find no dealer through whom to sell, and the consumer can get no oil but that of the monopoly. Price and quality are both thenceforth such as the combination chooses to make them. There are bargains in oil, but one party makes both sides of them. "We do not wish to ruin you without giving you another chance," said an agent of the combination gently to a merchant who persisted in selling opposition oil. "Look at this map; we have the country divided into districts. If you insist on war we will cut the prices in your territory to any necessary extent to destroy you, but we lose nothing. We simply make a corresponding advance in some other district. You lose everything. We cannot by any possibility lose anything."

[6] Testimony, Trusts, Congress, 1888, pp. 609-10.
[7] Ibid., p. 732.
[8] Ibid., p. 735.

XXXI

All the World Under One Hat

The reports of the United States consul-general at Berlin, in 1891, transmitted many interesting articles from the German papers concerning the alliance which it was believed had been made between the Rothschilds and the American oil combination. A company managed by the great bankers has obtained a commanding position in the Russian oil business, and the American and the Russian were even then said to have divided the world between them. The Berlin *Vossische Zeitung* said: "Heretofore the two petroleum speculators have marched apart, in order to get into their hands the two largest petroleum districts in the world. After this has been accomplished they unite to fight in unison, and to fix as they please the selling price for the whole world, which they divide between themselves. So an international speculating ring stands before the door, such as in like might and capital power has never before existed, and everywhere the intelligible fear prevails that within a short time the price of an article of use indispensable to all classes of people will rise with a bound, without its being possible for national legislation or control to raise any obstacles." [1]

The latest news in the summer of 1894 is of a great combination of Russian and American oil interests, under the direction of the Russian Minister of Finance, for a division of territory, regulation of prices, and the like. Information of this was given to the world by that minister's official organ in November, 1893. Thus says the Hanover (Germany) *Courier* of November 11th: "With the direct sanction of the Russian government the management of the enor-

[1] Translation from the Berlin *Vossische Zeitung*, June 12, 1891, Report of Consul-General Edwards, of Berlin.

mous wealth that lies in the yearly production of Russian petroleum will be concentrated in the hands of a few firms. . . . The
Russian government lends its hand for the formation of a trust
that reaches over the ocean—a trust, under State protection, against
the large mass of consumers. This is the newest acquisition of our
departing century."

It was announced that, in pursuance of this plan, the Russians
were to be given exclusive control of certain Asiatic markets. The
officers of the American combination are not easily reached by
newspaper men. But when this news came long interviews with
them were circulated in the press of the leading cities, dwelling
upon the "Waterloo" defeat they had suffered, and reassuring the
people with this evidence that there was, after all, "no monopoly."
The Russian interests are dominated by the Rothschilds, and if the
Rothschilds are, as these European observers declare, merely the
agents of the Americans, even unsophisticated people can understand the cheerfulness with which the trustees in New York dilate
on their Waterloo at the hands of their other self. Only this could
make credible the report that the world has been divided with
the Russians by our American "trustees," who never divide with
anybody. In dividing with the Russians they are dividing with
themselves.

Though it is reported that discriminations by the government
railroads of Russia were used to force the Russian producers into
this international trust, still, at worst, every Russian producer was
given by his government the right to enter the pool. But no
similar right for the American producer is recognized by our trust.
It admits only its own members. The others must "sell or squeeze."
There is something in the world more cruel than Russian despotism
—American "private enterprise."

One of the conditions said to have been made by the Russian
government is the natural one that the American trust, as it has
agreed to do for the French, must protect its Russian allies from
any competition from America. Extinction of the "independents"
has therefore become more important than ever to the trust. The
prize of victory over them is not only supremacy in this country,
but on four other continents. This will explain the new zeal with
which the suppression of the last vestige of American independence
in this industry has been sought the last few months of 1893 and
in 1894. Especially strenuous has been the renewal of the attack

on the pipe line the independents are seeking to lay to tidewater, and which they have carried as far as Wilkesbarre.

That pipe line, as it is the last hope of the people, is the greatest menace to the monopoly. The independents, as they have shown by the fact of surviving, although they have to pay extraordinary freights and other charges from which the trust is free, can produce more cheaply than the would-be Lords of Industry, as free men always do.[2] By means of this pipe line, suspended though it is at Wilkesbarre, are now made the only independent exports of oil that go from America to Europe. Once let the "outsiders" with their line reach the sea-shore and its open roads to the coast of America and Europe, and it will be a long chase they will give their pursuers. Everything that can be brought to bear by market manipulation, litigation, and other means is now being done to prevent the extension of this line, and bankrupt the men who are building it through much tribulation. The mechanical fixation of values, by which the refiners who use this line to export oil are compelled to meet a lower price for the refined in New York that can be got for the crude out of which it is made, has been already referred to, and, as shown above, the same prestidigitation of prices is being resorted to in Europe against the independents of Germany.

Early in 1894 the independent refiners and producers resolved to consolidate with this pipe line some other lines owned by them in order to strengthen and perfect the system, and put it in better shape to be extended to tide-water. This consolidation was voted by a large majority both of stock and stockholders. But a formidable opposition to it was at once begun in the courts by injunction proceedings in behalf of one man, a subordinate stockholder in a corporation of which the control is owned, as he admitted in court, by members of the oil trust.[3] The real litigant behind him, the independents stated to the court, was the same that we have seen appear in almost every chapter of our story, with its brigades of lawyers. "An unlawful organization," the independent described it to the court, "exercising great and illegal powers, . . . and bitterly and vindictively hostile to our business interests." They came into court one after the other and described the ruin which had

---

[2] See chs. xi. and xxx.
[3] Testimony of J. J. Carter in the case of J. J. Carter *vs.* Producers and Refiners' Oil Company, Limited. Court of Common Pleas Crawford County, Pa. May Term, 1894.

been wrought among them, telling the story the reader has found in these pages.

"It is our hope," they said, "when we once reach the salt-water that there will be no power there controlling the winds and the waves, the tides and the sun and moon, except the Power that controls everything. When we once are there the same forces that guide the ships of this monopoly to the farther shore will guide ours. The same winds that waft them will waft ours. There is freedom, there is hope, and there is the only chance of relief to this country. . . . Through three years of suffering and agony we have attempted to carry on our purpose. . . . You could have seen the blood-marks in the snow of the blood of the people who are working out their subscription as daily laborers on that line with nothing else to offer."

The injunctions asked for by this opposition were granted by the lower court, but the independents took an appeal to the Supreme Court of Pennsylvania. They first placed their petition for the rehearing in the hands of the chief-justice on Thursday, May 24th; on Monday, May 28th, the petition was renewed before the full court; on Thursday, May 31st, the court adjourned for the summer without taking any action upon the petition. The court in July agreed to hear the case at the opening of its next term, the first Monday of October. Section II. of Article I. of the Constitution of Pennsylvania says: "All courts shall be open, and every man, for an injury done him in his lands, goods, persons, or reputation, shall have remedy by due course of law, and right and justice administered, without sale, denial, or delay." To guard against the injustice which might arise by the granting of special injunctions by the lower courts—like that granted in this case—which might remain for months without remedy, the Legislature, in 1866, enacted a law which reads as follows: "In all cases in equity, in which a special injunction has been or shall be granted by any Court of Common Pleas, an appeal to the Supreme Court for the proper district shall be allowed, and all such appeals shall be heard by the Supreme Court in any district in which it may be in session."

As if there had not been enough to try these men, misfortune marked them in other ways. The Bradford refinery of the president of their pipe line was visited by a destructive fire during these proceedings in court. The Associated Press despatches attributed the fire to "spontaneous combustion," whatever that may be. But in another newspaper an eye-witness described how he saw a man running about the works in a mysterious way just before the flames broke out. On the same day, by a coincidence, the main pipe of the independent line was cut, and the oil, which spouted out to the tree-tops, was set on fire at a point in a valley where the greatest possible damage would result, and the telegraph wires were simultaneously cut, so that prompt repairs or salvage of oil were impossible. The Almighty is said to favor the heaviest battalions, and accident, if there is such a thing, seems to have the same preference, as has been shown in many incidents in our history, such as the mishaps to the Tidewater pipe line, and the Toledo municipal gas line.

XXXIII

The Smokeless Rebate

With searching intelligence, indomitable will, and a conscience which makes religion, patriotism, and the domestic virtues but subordinate paragraphs in a ritual of money worship, the mercantile mind flies its air-line to business supremacy. That entirely modern social arrangement—the private ownership of public highways—has introduced a new weapon into business warfare which means universal dominion to him who will use it with an iron hand.

This weapon is the rebate, smokeless, noiseless, invisible, of extraordinary range, and the deadliest gun known to commercial warfare. It is not a lawful weapon. Like the explosive bullet, it is not recognized by the laws of war. It has to be used secretly. All the rates he got were a secret between himself and the railroads. "It has never been otherwise," testified one of the oil combination.[1] The Chevalier Bayard declared proudly, as he lay on his death-bed, that he had never given quarter to any one so degraded and unknightly as to use gunpowder. Every one would close in at once to destroy a market combatant who avowed that he employed this wicked projectile.

The apparatus of the rebate is so simple that it looks less like a destroying angel than any weapon of offence ever known. The whole battery consists only of a pen and ink and some paper. The discharge is but the making of an entry—but the signing of a check. But when the man who commands this simple enginery directs it against a business competitor you can follow the track of wreckage like the path of a cyclone, by the ruins which lie bleaching in the air for years. The gentlemen who employ it give no

[1] Testimony, New York Assembly "Hepburn" Report, 1879, p. 2668.

evidence of being otherwise engaged than in their ordinary pur-
suits. They go about sedate and smiling, with seemingly friendly
hands empty of all tools of death. But all about them as they will,
as if it were only by wish of theirs which attendant spirits hastened
to execute, rivals are blown out of the highways, busy mills and
refineries turn to dust, hearts break, and strong men go mad or
commit suicide or surrender their persons and their property to
the skilful artillerists.

"And in the actual practice of daily life," says Ruskin, "you will
find that wherever there is secrecy, there is either guilt or danger."
"When did you discover the fact that these rebates had been paid?"
one of the victims was asked.

"We never discovered it as a fact until the testimony was taken
in 1879. . . . We always suspected it; but we never knew of it of
our personal knowledge, and never would really have known it of
our personal knowledge. . . . I had no idea of the iniquity that
was going on."[2]

The question most often pressed before all the many legislative
and judicial inquests held upon the dead bodies which strew every
field of the oil industry has been whether the extraordinary powers
which the invention of the locomotive and the transformation of
public highways into private property had given railways over the
livelihoods of the people had been used to make it impossible
for any but a preferred few to live.

One of the successful men disposed of the evidence that these
powers had been so used by styling it before the committee of
Congress of 1888 as the "worst balderdash," and before the New
York Legislative Committee of 1888 as "irresponsible newspaper
statement," "a malignity and mendacity that is little short of devil-
ishness." The secretary of the oil trust waved it away as "all this
newspaper talk and flurry." The president knows nothing about
the existence of such privileges, except that he has "heard much
of it in the papers." And yet another of the trust in the *North
American Review* of February, 1883, similarly describes the accusation as "uncontradicted calumny," to which, he regrets to say,
"several respectable journals and magazines lent themselves."

After taking 3700 pages of evidence and sitting for months, the
committee of 1879 of the New York Legislature said in their report: "The history of this corporation is a unique illustration of
the possible outgrowth of the present system of railroad manage-

[2] Testimony, Trusts, Congress, 1888, pp. 215, 223, 226.

ment in giving preferential rates, and also showing the colossal proportions to which monopoly can grow under the laws of this country.[3] . . . The parties whom they have driven to the wall have had ample capital and equal ability in the prosecution of their business in all things save their ability to acquire facilities for transportation." [4]

More than any others the wrongs of the oil industry provoked the investigations by Congress from 1872 to 1887, and caused the establishment of the Interstate Commerce Commission, and more than any others they have claimed the attention of the new law and the new court. The cases brought before it cover the oil business on practically every road of any importance in the United States—in New England, the Middle States, the West, the South, the Pacific coast; on the great East and West trunk roads—the Pennsylvania, the Erie, the Baltimore and Ohio, the New York Central, and all their allied lines; on the transcontinental lines—the Union Pacific, the Central Pacific, the Southern Pacific; on the steamship and railroad association controlling the South and Southwest. They show that from ocean to ocean, and from the Gulf of St. Lawrence to the Gulf of Mexico, wherever the American citizen seeks an opening in this industry, he finds it, like the deer forests and grouse moors of the old country, protected by game-keepers against him and the common herd. The terms in which the commission have described the preferences given the oil combination are not ambiguous: "Great difference in rates," "unjust discrimination," "intentional disregard of rights," "unexcused," "a vast discrepancy," "enormous," "illegal," "excessive," [5] "extraordinary," "forbidden by the act to regulate commerce," [6] "so obvious and palpable a discrimination that no discussion of it is necessary," "wholly indefensible," "patent and provoking discriminations for which no rational excuse is suggested," "obnoxious," "disparity . . . absurd and inexcusable," "gross disproportions and inequalities," [7] "long practised," "the most unjust and injurious discrimination . . . and this dis-

---

[3] New York Assembly "Hepburn" Report, 1879, pp. 40-41.

[4] *Ibid.*, p. 44.

[5] Rice *vs.* Louisville and Nashville Railroad *et al.* Interstate Commerce Commission Reports, vol. i, p. 722. Trusts, Congress, 1888, pp. 675-84.

[6] Scofield *vs.* Lake Shore and Michigan Southern Railroad. Interstate Commerce Commission Reports, vol. ii, p. 90.

[7] Rice, Robinson and Witherop *vs.* Western New York and Pennsylvania Railroad *et al.* Interstate Commerce Commission Reports, vol. iv., p. 131.

crimination inured mostly to the benefit of one powerful combination." [8]

This was what the Interstate Commerce Commission found all along the record from 1887 to 1893. When one of those who got the benefits so characterized was before the New York Legislature in 1888, he said:

"I know of no discrimination in the oil traffic of any kind since the passage of the Interstate Commerce Act."

"Do you use any means for the purpose of avoiding the effect of that new law?"

"None whatever." [9]

The general traffic manager of the Union Pacific Railroad said: "We have paid them a good deal in rebates." It was a "pretty large" preference.

"What was the effect on the small dealer?"

"I should think it would be embarrassing to the small shipper!" [10]

When the Interstate Commerce law went into force the oil combination introduced a patented car for the transcontinental trade, which it claimed the sole right to use. Though the new car was to the disadvantage of the railroads, as it cost more to haul, the managers gave it lower rates than any other car and carried it back free, while they punished the shippers who gave them a lighter and better car by charging them $105 for carrying that back.

A case now pending before the Interstate Commerce Commission, in which charges of highway abuse even more sensational than any of those we have seen judicially proved are made against the thirty railroads by which the oil of Ohio, Pennsylvania, and New York reaches the Pacific Coast. A San Francisco oil dealer is the petitioner for relief. Wm. C. Bissel vs. Atchison, Topeka and Santa Fé Railroad Company *et al.*

The San Francisco complainant goes on to charge that a plan was concocted and put in operation by which rates were lowered whenever the combination wanted to fill its warehouses on the Pacific coast, and as soon as they were full were put back again. This lowering and raising of rates was "to the public sudden and unexpected." [11] It was known in advance only to the ring and the

[8] *Ibid.*

[9] Testimony, Trusts, New York Senate, 1888, p. 597.

[10] Testimony, United States Pacific Railway Commission Report, 1887, pp. 1132-33.

[11] See pp. 47, 168, 182.

railroads. Before other shippers could take advantage of the low
rates they would be raised again. The complainant recites that in
pursuance of this plan, after the combination had transferred to
the Pacific coast at the end of 1888 from its Eastern refineries all
it needed for the next season's business, the railroads advanced the
rates from 82½ cents a hundred pounds to $1.25. The next May
the railroads made a similar seesaw, and, he says, in December,
1892, "are still making . . . such arbitrary and sudden reductions
. . . to the undue advantage" of the oil combination "and to the
detriment and injury of all other shippers."

This is not all of the story. This patented car spoken of was a
mere aggregation of old elements, as the courts held, and the patent
was void. Advised by their lawyer, that this would be the view the
courts would have to take, competitors of the combination in the
business of the Pacific coast, where they had been at the head until
these new tricks of trade came in, introduced a car of their own of
the same class. They thus became entitled to the same low rates and
the same free return of the car as their powerful rival. This put
them again on an equality in transportation. They had not been
using these new cars long before two of them, shipped as usual
from the East, failed to arrive. Their search for the missing cars
put them in possession of the interesting information that a litigation, of which they had had no notice or knowledge whatever,
had for some time been in progress, and was at that moment at
the point of decision. As their interests had been entirely unrepre-
sented, this decision would certainly have been against them, and
would have forever made impossible the use of their cars on any
railroad of the United States. This had been done by an apparently
hostile litigation by the oil combination against the Southern
Pacific Railroad. The former sued in the United States courts for
an injunction to forbid the railroad from hauling the cars of the
competitor, on the ground that they were an infringement on its
own patented cars. No notice was given the persons most interested
—the owners of the cars in question—whose business life was involved, and they were not at first made parties to the suit. The
dummy defendant—the railroad—made no valid opposition, but
with great condescension admitted that all the averments of its
antagonist were true. The case was sent through the courts on a
gallop to get a decision. After that the merchants whose cars were
the object of the attack, as they had not been parties to the case,
could not have it reopened, and it would stand against them with-

out possibility of reversal. The firm found that a temporary injunction had been applied for and had been granted; that this had been followed by proceedings to make the injunction perpetual; that subpoenas had been issued, served, and returned, and an order had been obtained from the court for taking testimony. In place of the regular examiner of the court, a special examiner had been appointed; he had begun taking evidence the same day, and taking it privately. The testimony so taken had been sealed and filed. The railroad had made its answer December 2d, the testimony already taken was filed in court December 3d, making the case complete for decision by the judges. December 4th the firm heard for the first time of what was being done, and December 5th applied for the right to take part, which saved them. To get such cases ready for a hearing in the United States Circuit Court, where this was done, usually requires a year. But in this instance it was done in two weeks! Only just as the door of the court was closing irrevocably, as far as their rights were concerned, did the firm get inside, and secure leave to have their side represented. The whole fabric of the litigation fell at the first touch. The temporary injunction against the use of their car was dissolved, the permanent injunction was refused, the patent of the oil trust's car was declared worthless, and this decision was upheld by the United States Circuit Court of Appeals in February, 1893.[12]

Meanwhile their oil, side-tracked in the Mojave Desert and elsewhere, was being cooked to death, their customers were going elsewhere, and they were being put to loss and damages which they are now suing to have made good to them. "There are some equivocal circumstances in the case," said Judge Hoffman, dissolving the injunctions in 1890. He pointed out that the railroad made no objection to the injunction which deprived it of business. This "tends to corroborate suspicions," he said, suggested by other features of the case. The railroad persisted in remaining in the case to the end, after the real parties in interest came in, and, although codefendants with these parties, the road manoeuvred for the benefit of the other side in a way which the Court again said "had an equivocal appearance." The counsel for the firm, in his brief for the United States Circuit Court of Appeals, pointed out more causes for "suspicion." He showed the Court that the records of the case had been mutilated in many places. All the mutilations

[12] Standard Oil Company *vs.* Southern Pacific Railroad and Whittier, Fuller & Co., 48 *Federal Reporter*, p. 109.

were in favor of the other side of the case. Who was the author of
the mutilations was not shown, but it was shown that the record
had been intrusted by the lower court to a representative of one of
the oil trust, to be printed and delivered to the Court of Appeals.
"It would be a very easy matter for a vicious attorney," said the
lawyer of the independents, "under such circumstances, to make
changes and alterations in the record that might not be noticed,
but would nevertheless greatly prejudice the case."

As the counsel of the New York Chamber of Commerce before
the New York Legislative Committee of 1879 said: "Such a power
makes it possible to the freight agents of the railways to constitute
themselves special partners in every line of business in the United
States, contributing as their share of capital to the business the
ability to crush out rivals." Men who can choose which merchants,
manufacturers, producers shall go to market and which stay at
home, have a key that will unlock the door of every business house
on the line; they know the combination of every safe.

Some railroad men are known to have been stockholders in the
oil combination. "I think I owned—I guess I had $100,000 in
it . . . I don't know anything at all about it"—the company—
the head of the New York Central admitted.[13] Who were the
owners of certain shares of their capital stock these men have always
refused to divulge. In giving in court a list of stockholders of one of
their corporations one of the officers uncovered only three-quarters
of the stock. Who held the other fourth he avowed he could not
say, although the stock-book was in his custody.[14] The dividends
were paid to the vice-president, and by him handed over to these
veiled prophets. There was a similar mystery about the owners of
about $2,000,000 of the National Transit stock, the concern which
owns and manages the pipe lines. Asked for the names of the
owners of this portion, the "secretary" said:

"It is a private matter . . . I decline to answer." [15]

The smokeless rebate makes the secret of success in business to
be not manufacture, but manufracture—breaking down with a
strong hand the true makers of things. To those who can get the
rebate it makes no difference who does the digging, building, min-
ing, making, producing the million forms of the wealth they covet

[13] Testimony, New York Assembly "Hepburn" Report, 1879, pp. 1314-15.
[14] Testimony, Commonwealth of Pennsylvania vs. Pennsylvania Railroad, et al.,
1879, p. 529.
[15] Testimony, Trusts, Congress, 1888, pp. 367-68.

for themselves. They need only get control of the roads. All that they want of the wealth of others can be switched off the highways into their hands. To succeed, ambitious men must make themselves refiners of freight rates, distillers of discriminations, owners, not of lands, mines, and forests—not in the first place, at least—but of the railway officials through whose hands the produce must go to market; builders, not of manufactories, but of privileges; inventors only of schemes to keep for themselves the middle of the road and both sides of it; contrivers, not of competition, but of ways to tax the property of their competitors into their pockets. They need not make money; they can take it from those who have made it.

From using railroad power to give better rates to the larger man, it was an easy step to using it to make a favorite first a larger man, then the largest man, and finally the only man in the business. In meat and cattle we see men rising from poverty to great wealth. From being competitors, like other men, in the scramble, they get into the comfortable seat of control of the prices at which the farmer must sell cattle, and at which the people must buy meat.[16] Many other men had thrift, sobriety, industry, but only these had the rebate, and so only these are the "fittest in the struggle for existence." We find a merchant prince of the last generation in New York gathering into his hands a share of the dry-goods business of the country which appears entirely disproportionate to his ability and energy, great though these be. Is his secret a brain so much larger than his competitors' brains as his business is greater than theirs? The freight agent of the New York Central testified that he gave this man a special rate "to build up and develop their business."

"This," said the counsel for the Chamber of Commerce of New York before the commirtee, "is deliberately making the rich richer and the poor poorer, by taxing the poor for the benefit of the rich through the instrumentality of the freight charge." [17]

The officials of the Pennsylvania Railroad, by the use of rebates, handed over the State of Pennsylvania to three coal-dealers, each of whom had his territory, and was supreme in it, as would-be competitors found out when they undertook to ship coal into his market. They made a similar division of the iron and steel business. The rebate is the golden-rule of the "gospel of wealth." We

---

[16] Testimony, New York Assembly "Hepburn" Report, 1879, pp. 397, 781, 825, 924, 1383. United States Senate Report on Meat Products, p. 23.

[17] *Ibid.*, speech of Simon Sterne, p. 3996.

have already seen that the secret of the few corporations which
have become the owners of almost every acre of the anthracite coal
of Pennsylvania was the rebate.

Along one of the most important lines out of Chicago grain
dealers who had been buying and selling in an open market, building elevators, investing capital and life, found five years ago market and railroad and livelihood suddenly closed to them, and the
work of thirty years brought to an untimely end. The United
States Interstate Commerce Commission, and the United States District Attorneys co-operating with it, broke down in the attempt
to compel the railroad men who gave these privileges of transportation, or the business men who received them, to testify or to produce their books. The United States grand-jury in Chicago, in
December, 1890, proceeded against the shippers and the railroad
men. All of them refused to tell the rates given or received, or to
produce their books.

Why do you refuse to answer? they were asked.

Because to do so would incriminate us.

Public opinion, as yet only in the gristle in these new questions,
turns upon first one and then another as the author of its troubles
—the soulless corporation, the combination of corporations, railroad oppression, or what not. But the corporation is merely a
cover, the combination of corporations an advantage, the private
ownership of public highways an opportunity, and the rebate its
perfect tool. The real actors are men; the real instrument, the control of their fellows by wealth, and the mainspring of the evil is
the morals and economics which cipher that brothers produce
wealth when they are only cheating each other out of birthrights.

The success of the same men in Europe shows that railroad discrimination is not the essence of their power, though it has in
America been the chief instrument. By their wealth and their
willingness to use it in their way they have become supreme.
Supreme even where, as in England and Germany, they had no
such unjust and crushing preference on the highways as in America.
Back of highway privilege, back of money power, back of trade
supremacy gained by these two means must be reckoned, as the
essence of this phenomenon, the morality—our morality—which
not only allows but encourages men to do each other to death,
provided only the weapon be a bargain and the arena a market.
"Everything shall not go to market," says Emerson; but everything
does go to market. The millionaire is the modern hero, says the

New York *Evening Post*. The men who have found in the rebate the secret of business success—and there are more of them than the public guesses—have only extended a fiercer hand to the results all were aiming at. They have used the smokeless rebate because it was the best gun. But if that had not been ready to their hand, they would have taken the next best. The course of conquest might have been slower, but, unless checked by moral interventions, it would have reached the same end. If society is founded on the idea that property belongs to the strongest, these will sooner or later get all the property, by bargains or by battles according to "the spirit of the age."

XXXIV

The Old Self-Interest

The corn of the coming harvest is growing so fast that, like the farmer standing at night in his fields, we can hear it snap and crackle. We have been fighting fire on the well-worn lines of old-fashioned politics and political economy, regulating corporations, and leaving competition to regulate itself. But the flames of a new economic evolution run around us, and we turn to find that competition has killed competition, that corporations are grown greater than the State and have bred individuals greater than themselves, and that the naked issue of our time is with property becoming master instead of servant, property in many necessaries of life becoming monopoly of the necessaries of life.

We are still, in part, as Emerson says, in the quadruped state. Our industry is a fight of every man for himself. The prize we give the fittest is monopoly of the necessaries of life, and we leave these winners of the powers of life and death to wield them over us by the same "self-interest" with which they took them from us. In all this we see at work a "principle" which will go into the records as one of the historic mistakes of humanity. Institutions stand or fall by their philosophy, and the main doctrine of industry since Adam Smith has been the fallacy that the self-interest of the individual was a sufficient guide to the welfare of the individual and society. Heralded as a final truth of "science" this proves to have been nothing higher than a temporary formula for a passing problem. It was a reflection in words of the policy of the day.

When the Middle Ages landed on the shores of the sixteenth century they broke ranks, and for three hundred years every one has been scurrying about to get what he could. Society was not

highly developed enough to organize the exploration and subju-
gation of worlds of new things and ideas on any broader basis than
private enterprise, personal adventure. People had to run away
from each other and from the old ideas, nativities, guilds, to seize
the prizes of the new sciences, the new land, the new liberties which
make modern times. They did not go because the philosophers told
them to. The philosophers saw them going and wrote it down in
a book, and have believed themselves ever since to be the inventors
of the division of labor and the discoverers of a new world of
social science. But now we are touching elbows again, and the
dream of these picnic centuries that the social can be made secondary to the individual is being chased out of our minds by the
hard light of the crisis into which we are waking.

"It is a law of business for each proprietor to pursue his own
interest," said the committee of Congress which in 1893 investigated
the coal combinations. "There is no hope for any of us, but the
weakest must go first," is the golden rule of business.[1] There is no
other field of human associations in which any such rule of action
is allowed. The man who should apply in his family or his citizenship this "survival of the fittest" theory as it is practically professed
and operated in business would be a monster, and would be speedily
made extinct, as we do with monsters. To divide the supply of
food between himself and his children according to their relative
powers of calculation, to follow his conception of his own self-interest in any matter which the self-interest of all has taken charge
of, to deal as he thinks best for himself with foreigners with whom
his country is at war, would be a short road to the penitentiary or
the gallows. In trade men have not yet risen to the level of the
family life of the animals. The true law of business is that all
must pursue the interest of all. In the law, the highest product of
civilization, this has long been a commonplace. The safety of the
people is the supreme law. We are in travail to bring industry up
to this. Our century of the caprice of the individual as the law-
giver of the common toil, to employ or disemploy, to start or
stop, to open or close, to compete or combine, has been the disorder of the school while the master slept. The happiness, self-
interest, or individuality of the whole is not more sacred than
that of each, but it is greater. They are equal in quality, but in
quantity they are greater. In the ultimate which the mathematician,
the poet, the reformer projects the two will coincide.

[1] Testimony. Trusts, Congress, 1888, p. 215.

Meanwhile, we who are the creators of society have got the times out of joint, because, less experienced than the Creator of the balanced matter of earth, we have given the precedence to the powers on one side. As gods we are but half-grown. For a hundred years or so our economic theory has been one of industrial government by the self-interest of the individual. Political government by the self-interest of the individual we call anarchy. It is one of the paradoxes of public opinion that the people of America, least tolerant of this theory of anarchy in political government, lead in practising it in industry. Politically, we are civilized; industrially, not yet. Our century, given to this *laissez-faire*—"leave the individual alone; he will do what is best for himself, and what is best for him is best for all"—has done one good: it has put society at the mercy of its own ideals, and has produced an actual anarchy in industry which is horrifying us into a change of doctrines.

The true *laissez-faire* is, let the individual do what the individual can do best, and let the community do what the community can do best. The *laissez-faire* of social self-interest, if true, cannot conflict with the individual self-interest, if true, but it must outrank it always. What we have called "free competition" has not been free, only freer than what went before. The free is still to come. The pressure we feel is notice to prepare for it. Civilization—the process of making men citizens in their relations to each other, by exacting of each that he give to all that which he receives from all—has reached only those forms of common effort which, because most general and most vital, first demanded its harmonizing touch. Men joining in the labors of the family, the mutual sacrifices of the club or the church in the union of forces for self-defence and for the gains of co-operation on the largest scale in labors of universal concern, like letter-carrying, have come to be so far civilized.

Where the self-interest of the individual is allowed to be the rule both of social and personal action, the level of all is forced down to that of the lowest. Business excuses itself for the things it does—cuts in wages, exactions in hours, tricks of competition—on the plea that the merciful are compelled to follow the cruel. "It is pleaded as an excuse by those" (common carriers) "who desire to obey the" (Interstate Commerce) "law that self-preservation drives them to violate it because other carriers persist in doing so," says Senator Cullom.[2] When the self-interest of society

---

[2] Cullom: Shelby M. Cullom (1829-1914), American politician, was U.S. Senator who helped sponsor the Interstate Commerce Act of 1887. [T.C.]

is made the standard the lowest must rise to the average. The one pulls down, the other up. That men's hearts are bad and that bad men will do bad things has a truth in it. But whatever the general average of morals, the anarchy which gives such individuals their head and leaves them to set the pace for all will produce infinitely worse results than a policy which applies mutual checks and inspirations. Bad kings make bad reigns, but monarchy is bad because it is arbitrary power, and that, whether it be political or industrial, makes even good men bad.

A partial truth universally applied as this of self-interest has been is a universal error. Everything goes to defeat. Highways are used to prevent travel and traffic. Ownership of the means of production is sought in order to "shut down" production, and the means of plenty make famine. All follow self-interest to find that though they have created marvellous wealth it is not theirs. We pledge "our lives, our fortunes, and our sacred honor" to establish the rule of the majority, and end by finding that the minority—a minority in morals, money, and men—are our masters whichever way we turn. We agonize over "economy," but sell all our grain and pork and oil and cotton at exchanges where we pay brokerage on a hundred or a thousand barrels or bushels or bales of wind to get one real one sold. These intolerabilities—sweat-shops where model merchants buy and sell the cast-off scarlet-fever skins of the poor, factory and mine where childhood is forbidden to become manhood and manhood is forbidden to die a natural death, mausoleums in which we bury the dead rich, slums in which we bury the living poor, coal pools with their manufacture of artificial winter—all these are the rule of private self-interest arrived at its destination.

A really human life is impossible in our cities, but they cannot be reconstructed under the old self-interest. Chicago was rebuilt wrong after the fire. Able men pointed out the avenues to a wider and better municipal life, but they could not be opened through the private interpositions that blocked the way. The slaughter of railway men coupling cars was shown, in a debate in the United States Senate, to be twice as great as it would be if the men were in active service in war. But under the scramble for private gain our society on its railway side cannot develop the energy to introduce the improved appliances ready at hand which would save these lives, all young and vigorous. The cost of the change would be repaid in 100-per-cent. dividends every year by the money value alone to us of the men now killed and wounded. But we shall have to wait for a nobler arithmetic to give us investments so good as that. The lean kine of self-interest devour the fat kine.

We are very poor. The striking feature of our economic condition is our poverty, not our wealth. We make ourselves "rich" by appropriating the property of others by methods which lessen the total property of all. Spain took such riches from America and grew poor. Modern wealth more and more resembles the winnings of speculators in bread during famine—worse, for to make the money it makes the famine. What we call cheapness shows itself to be unnatural fortunes for a very few, monstrous luxury for them and proportionate deprivation for the people, judges debauched, trustees dishonored, Congress and State legislatures insulted and defied, when not seduced, multitudes of honest men ruined and driven to despair, the common carrier made a mere instrument for the creation of a new baronage, an example set to hundreds of would-be commercial Caesars to repeat this rapine in other industries and call it "business," a process set in operation all over the United States for the progressive extinction of the independence of laboring men, and all business men except the very rich, and their reduction to a state of vassalage to lords or squires in each department of trade and industry. All these—tears, ruin, dishonor, and treason—are the unmarked additions to the "price marked on the goods."

Syndicates, by one stroke, get the power of selling dear on one side, and producing cheap on the other. Thus they keep themselves happy, prices high, and the people hungry. What model merchant could ask more? The dream of the king who wished that all his people had but one neck that he might decapitate them at one blow is realized to-day in this industrial garrote. The syndicate has but to turn its screw, and every neck begins to break. Prices paid to such intercepters are not an exchange of service; they are ransom paid by the people for their lives. The ability of the citizen to pay may fluctuate; what he must pay remains fixed, or advances like the rent of the Irish tenant to the absentee landlord until the community interfered. Those who have this power to draw the money from the people—from every railroad station, every street-car, every fireplace, every salt-cellar, every bread-pan, wash-board, and coal-scuttle—to their own safes have the further incentive to make this money worth the most possible. By contracting the issue of currency and contracting it again by hoarding it in their banks, safe-deposit vaults, and the government treasury, they can depress the prices of all that belongs to the people. Their own prices are fixed. These are "regular prices," established by price-lists. Given, as a ruling motive, the principles of business—to get the most and give the least; given the legal and economic, physical and mechanical control, possible under our present social arrangements, to the few over the many, and the certain end of all this, if unarrested, unreversed, can be nothing less than a return to chattel slavery. There may be some finer name, but the fact will not be finer. Between our present tolerance and our completed subjection the distance is not so far as that from the equality and simplicity of our Pilgrim Fathers to ourselves.

Everything withers—even charity. Aristocratic benevolence spends a shrunken stream in comparison with democratic benevolence. In an address to the public, soliciting subscriptions, the Committee of the United Hospitals Association of New York said, in December, 1893: "The committee have found that, through the obliteration of old methods of individual competition by the establishment of large corporations and trusts in modern times, the income of such charitable institutions as are supported by the individual gifts of the benevolent has been seriously affected."

In the worst governments and societies that have existed one good can be seen—so good that the horrors of them fall back into secondary places as extrinsic, accidental. That good is the ability of men to lead the life together. The more perfect monopoly makes itself the more does it bring into strong lights the greatest fact of our industry, of far more permanent value than the greed which has for the moment made itself the cynosure of all eyes. It makes this fair world more fair to consider the loyalties, intelligences, docilities of the multitudes who are guarding, developing, operating with the faithfulness of brothers and the keen interest of owners properties and industries in which brotherhood is not known and their title is not more than a tenancy at will. One of the largest stones in the arch of "consolidation," perhaps the keystone, is that men have become so intelligent, so responsive and responsible, so co-operative that they can be intrusted in great masses with the care of vast properties owned entirely by others and with the operation of complicated processes, although but a slender cost of subsistence is awarded them out of fabulous profits. The spectacle of the million and more employés of the railroads of this country despatching trains, maintaining tracks, collecting fares and freights, and turning over hundreds of millions of net profits to the owners, not one in a thousand of whom would know how to do the simplest of these things for himself, is possible only where civilization has reached a high average of morals and culture. More and more the mills and mines and stores, and even the farms and forests, are being administered by others than the owners. The virtue of the people is taking the place Poor Richard thought only the eye of the owner could fill. If mankind, driven by their fears and the greed of others, can do so well, what will be their productivity and cheer when the "interest of all" sings them to their work?

This new morality and new spring of wealth have been seized first by the appropriating ones among us. But, as has been in government, their intervention of greed is but a passing phase. Mankind belongs to itself, not to kings or monopolists, and will supersede the one as surely as the other with the institutions of democracy. Yes, Callicles, said Socrates, the greatest are usually the bad, for they have the power. If power could continue paternal and benign, mankind would not be rising through one emancipation after another into a progressive communion of equalities. The individual and society will always be wrestling with each other in a composition of forces. But to just the extent to which civilization prevails, society will be held as inviolable as the individual; not subordinate—indeed inaudible—as now in the counting-room and corporation-office. We have overworked the self-interest of the individual. The line of conflict between individual and social is a progressive one of the discovery of point after point in which the two are identical. Society thus passes from conflict to harmony, and on to another conflict. Civilization is the unceasing accretion of these social solutions. We fight out to an equilibrium, as in the abolition of human slavery; then upon this new level thus built up we enter upon the struggle for a new equilibrium, as now in the labor movement. The man for himself destroys himself and all men; only society can foster him and them.

Children yet, we run everything we do—love or war, work or leisure, religion or liberty—to excess. Every possibility of body and mind must be played upon till it is torn to pieces, as toys by children. Priests, voluptuaries, tyrants, knights, ascetics—in the long procession of fanatics a new-comer takes his place; he is called "the model merchant"—the cruelest fanatic in history. He is the product of ages given to progressive devotion to "trading." He is the high-priest of the latest idolatry, the self-worship of self-interest.

Whirling-dirvish of the market, self, friends, and family, body and soul, loves, hopes, and faith, all are sacrificed to seeing how many "turns" he can make before he drops dead. Trade began, Sir Henry Sumner Maine[3] tells us, not within the family or community, but without. Its first appearances are on the neutral borderland between hostile tribes. There, in times of peace, they meet to trade, and think it no sin that "the buyer must beware" since the buyer is an enemy. Trade has spread thence, carrying with itself into family and State the poison of enmity. From the fatherhood of the old patriarchal life, where father and brother sold each other nothing, the world has chaffered along to the anarchy of a "free" trade which sells everything. One thing after another has passed out from under the regime of brotherhood and passed in under that of bargainhood. The ground we move on, the bodies we work with, and the necessaries we live by are all being "exchanged," by "rules fetched with cupidity from heartless schools," into the ownership of the Jacobs of mankind. By these rules the cunning are the good, and the weak and the tender the bad, and the good are to have all the goods and the weak are to have nothing. These rules give one the power to supply or deny work to thousands, and to use the starvation terms of the men he disemploys as the measure of the cost of subsistence of all workmen. This must be near the end. The very churches have become mercantilized, and are markets in which "prophets" are paid fancy prices—"always called of God," as Milton said, "but always to a greater benefice"—and worshippers buy and sell knee-room.

Conceptions of duty take on a correspondingly unnatural complexion. The main exhortations the world gives beginners are how to "get on"—the getting on so ardently inculcated being to get, like the old-man-of-the-sea, on somebody's back. "If war fails you in the country where you are, you must go where there is war," said one of the successful men of the fourteenth century to a young knight who asked him for the Laws of Life. "I shall be perfectly satisfied with you," I heard one of the great business geniuses of America say to his son, "if you will only always go to bed at night worth more than when you got up in the morning." The system grows, as all systems do, more complicated, and gets further away from its first purposes of barter of real things and services. It goes more under the hands

---

[3] Maine: Sir Henry Sumner Maine (1822-1888). English jurist and historian of the law and comparative institutions. His most famous work is *Ancient Law.* [T.C.]

of men of apt selfishness, who push it further away from general comprehension and the general good. Tariffs, currencies, finances, freight-rate sheets, the laws, become instruments of privilege, and just in proportion become puzzles no people can decipher. "I have a right to buy my labor where I can buy it cheapest"—beginning as a protest against the selfish exclusions of antiquated trade-guilds outgrown by the new times—has at last come to mean, "I have a right to do anything to cheapen the labor I want to buy, even to destroying the family life of the people."

When steaming kettles grew into beasts of burden and public highways dwindled into private property administered by private motives for private ends, all previous tendencies were intensified into a sudden whirl redistributing wealth and labors. It appears to have been the destiny of the railroad to begin and of oil to lubricate to its finish the last stage of this crazy commercialism. Business colors the modern world as war reddened the ancient world. Out of such delirium monsters are bred, and their excesses destroy the system that brought them forth. There is a strong suggestion of moral insanity in the unrelieved sameness of mood and unvarying repetition of one act in the life in the model merchant. Sane minds by an irresistible law alternate one tension with another. Only a lunatic is always smiling or always weeping or always clamoring for dividends. Eras show their last stages by producing men who sum up individually the morbid characteristics of the mass. When the crisis comes in which the gathering tendencies of generations shoot forward in the avalanche, there is born some group of men perfect for their function—good be it or bad. They need to take time for no second thought, and will not delay the unhalting reparations of nature by so much as the time given to one tear over the battle-field or the bargain. With their birth their mission is given them, whether it be the mission of Lucifer or Gabriel. This mission becomes their conscience. The righteous indignation that other men feel against sin these men feel against that which withstands them. Sincere as rattlesnakes, they are selfish with the unconsciousness possible to only the entirely common place, without the curiosity to question their times or the imagination to conceive the pain they inflict, and their every ideal is satisfied by the conventionalities of church, parlor, and counting-room. These men are the touchstones to wither the cant of an age.

We preach "Do as you would be done by" in our churches, and "A fair exchange no robbery" in our counting-rooms, and "All citi-

zens are equal as citizens" in courts and Congress. Just as we are
in danger of believing that to say these things is to do them and be
them, there come unto us these men, practical as granite and gravi-
tation. Taking their cue not from our lips, but from our lives, they
better the instruction, and, passing easily to the high seats at every
table, prove that we are liars and hypocrites. Their only secret is
that they do, better than we, the things we are all trying to do, but
of which in our morning and evening prayers, seen of all men, we
are continually making believe to pray: Good Lord, deliver us!
When the hour strikes for such leaders, they come and pass as by a
law of nature to the front. All follow them. It is their fate and ours
that they must work out to the end the destiny interwoven of their
own insatiate ambition and the false ideals of us who have created
them and their opportunity.

If our civilization is destroyed, as Macaulay predicted, it will not
be by his barbarians from below. Our barbarians come from above.
Our great money-makers have sprung in one generation into seats
of power kings do not know. The forces and the wealth are new,
and have been the opportunity of new men. Without restraints of
culture, experience, the pride, or even the inherited caution of class
or rank, these men, intoxicated, think they are the wave instead of
the float, and that they have created the business which has created
them. To them science is but a never-ending repertoire of investments stored up by nature for the syndicates, government but a
fountain of franchises, the nations but customers in squads, and a
million the unit of a new arithmetic of wealth written for them.
They claim a power without control, exercised through forms which
make it secret, anonymous, and perpetual. The possibilities of its
gratification have been widening before them without interruption
since they began, and even at a thousand millions they will feel
no satiation and will see no place to stop. They are gluttons of
luxury and power, rough, unsocialized, believing that mankind must
be kept terrorized. Powers of pity die out of them, because they
work through agents and die in their agents, because what they do
is not for themselves.

Of gods, friends, learnings, of the uncomprehended civilization
they overrun, they ask but one question: How much? What is a
good time to sell? What is a good time to buy? The Church and the
Capitol, incarnating the sacrifices and triumphs of a procession of
martyrs and patriots since the dawn of freedom, are good enough
for a money-changer's shop for them, and a market and shambles.

Their heathen eyes see in the law and its consecrated officers nothing but an intelligence-office and hired men to help them burglarize the treasures accumulated for thousands of years at the altars of liberty and justice, that they may burn their marbles for the lime of commerce.

Business motivated by the self-interest of the individual runs into monopoly at every point it touches the social life—land monopoly, transportation monopoly, trade monopoly, political monopoly in all its forms, from contraction of the currency to corruption in office. The society in which in half a lifetime a man without a penny can become a hundred times a millionaire is as over-ripe, industrially, as was, politically, the Rome in which the most popular bully could lift himself from the ranks of the legion on to the throne of the Caesars. Our rising issue is with business. Monopoly is business at the end of its journey. It has got there. The irrepressible conflict is now as distinctly with business as the issue so lately met was with slavery. Slavery went first only because it was the cruder form of business.

Our tyrants are our ideals incarnating themselves in men born to command. What these men are we have made them. All governments are representative governments; none of them more so than our government of industry. We go hopelessly astray if we seek the solution of our problems in the belief that our business rulers are worse men in kind than ourselves. Worse in degree; yes. It is a race to the bad, and the winners are the worst. A system in which the prizes go to meanness invariably marches with the meanest men at the head. But if any could be meaner than the meanest it would be they who run and fail and rail.

Every idea finds its especially susceptible souls. These men are our most susceptible souls to the idea of individual self-interest. They have believed implicitly what we have taught, and have been the most faithful in trying to make the talent given them grow into ten talents. They rise superior to our half-hearted social corrections: publicity, private competition, all devices of market-opposition, private litigation, public investigation, legislation, and criminal prosecution—all. Their power is greater to-day than it was yesterday, and will be greater to-morrow. The public does not withhold its favor, but deals with them, protects them, refuses to treat their crimes as it treats those of the poor, and admits them to the highest places. The predominant mood is the more or less concealed regret of the citizens that they have not been able to conceive and execute the same lucky stroke or some other as profitable. The conclusion is irresistible that men so given the lead are the representatives of the real "spirit of the age," and that the protestants against them are not representative of our times—are at best but intimators of times which may be.

Two social energies have been in conflict, and the energy of reform has so far proved the weaker. We have chartered the self-interest of the individual as the rightful sovereign of conduct; we have taught that the scramble for profit is the best method of administering the riches of earth and the exchange of services. Only those can attack this system who attack its central principle, that strength gives the strong in the market the right to destroy his neighbor. Only as we have denied that right to the strong elsewhere have we made ourselves as civilized as we are. And we cannot make a change as long as our songs, customs, catchwords, and public opinion tell all to do the same thing if they can. Society, in each person of its multitudes, must recognize that the same principles of the interest of all being the rule of all, of the strong serving the weak, of the first being the last—"I am among you as one that serves"—which have given us the home where the weakest is the one surest of his rights and of the fullest service of the strongest, and have given us the republic in which all join their labor that the poorest may be fed, the weakest defended, and all educated and prospered, must be applied where men associate in common toil as wherever they associate. Not until then can the forces be reversed which generate those obnoxious persons—our fittest.

Our system, so fair in its theory and so fertile in its happiness and prosperity in its first century, is now, following the fate of systems, becoming artificial, technical, corrupt; and, as always happens in human institutions, after noon, power is stealing from the many to the few. Believing wealth to be good, the people believed the wealthy to be good. But, again in history, power has intoxicated and hardened its possessors, and Pharaohs are bred in counting-rooms as they were in palaces. Their furniture must be banished to the world-garret, where lie the out-worn trappings of the guilds and slavery and other old lumber of human institutions.

XXXV

And the New

The question is not whether monopoly is to continue. The sun sets every night on a greater majority against it. We are face to face with the practical issue: Is it to go through ruin or reform? Can we forestall ruin by reform? If we wait to be forced by events we shall be astounded to find how much more radical they are than our utopias. Louis XVI waited until 1793, and gave his head and all his investitures to the people who in 1789 asked only to sit at his feet and speak their mind. Unless we reform of our own free will, nature will reform us by force, as nature does. Our evil courses have already gone too far in producing misery, plagues, hatreds, national enervation. Already the leader is unable to lead, and has begun to drive with judges armed with bayonets and Gatling guns. History is the serial obituary of the men who thought they could drive men.

Reform is the science and conscience with which mankind in its manhood overcomes temptations and escapes consequences by killing the germs. Ruin is already hard at work among us. Our libraries are full of the official inquiries and scientific interpretations which show how our master-motive is working decay in all our parts. The family crumbles into a competition between the father and the children whom he breeds to take his place in the factory, to unfit themselves to be fathers in their turn. A thorough, stalwart resimplification, a life governed by simple needs and loves, is the imperative want of the world. It will be accomplished: either self-conscious volition does it, or the slow wreck and decay of superfluous and unwholesome men and matters. The latter is the method of brutes and brute civilizations. The other is the method of man, so far as he is divine. Has not man, who has in personal reform risen above the brute method, come to the height at which he can achieve social reform in masses and by nations? We must learn; we can learn by reason. Why wait for the crueler teacher?

We have a people like which none has ever existed before. We have millions capable of conscious co-operation. The time must come in social evolution when the people can organize the free will to choose salvation which the individual has been cultivating for 1900 years, and can adopt a policy more dignified and more effective than leaving themselves to be kicked along the path of reform by the recoil of their own vices. We must bring the size of our morality up to the size of our cities, corporations, and combinations, or these will be brought down to fit our half-grown virtue.

The break-down of all other civilizations has been a slow decay. It took the Northerners hundreds of years to march to the Tiber. They grew their way through the old society as the tree planting itself on a grave is found to have sent its roots along every fibre and muscle of the dead. Our world is not the simple thing theirs was, of little groups sufficient to themselves, if need be. New York would begin to die to-morrow if it were not for Illinois and Dakota. We cannot afford a revulsion in the hearts by whose union locomotives run, mills grind, factories make. Practical men are speculating to-day on the possibility that our civilization may some afternoon be flashed away by the tick of a telegraph. All these co-operations can be scattered by a word of hate too many, and we left, with no one who knows how to make a plough or a match, a civilization cut off as by the Roman curse from food and fire. Less sensitive civilizations than ours have burst apart.

Two classes study and practise politics and government: place hunters and privilege hunters. In a world of relativities like ours size of area has a great deal to do with the truth of principles. America has grown so big—and the tickets to be voted, and the powers of government, and the duties of citizens, and the profits of personal use of public functions have all grown so big—that the average citizen has broken down. No man can half understand or half operate the fulness of this big citizenship, except by giving his whole time to it. This the place hunter can do, and the privilege hunter. Government, therefore—municipal, State, national—is passing into the hands of these two classes, specialized for the functions of power by their appetite for the fruits of power. The power of citizenship is relinquished by those who do not and cannot know how to exercise it to those who can and do—by those who have a livelihood to make to those who make politics their livelihood.

These specialists of the ward club, the primary, the campaign, the election, and office unite, by a law as irresistible as that of the sexes, with those who want all the goods of government—charters, contracts, rulings, permits. From this marriage it is easy to imagine that among some other people than ourselves, and in some other century than this, the offspring might be the most formidable, elusive, unrestrained, impersonal, and cruel tyranny the world has yet seen. There might come a time when the policeman and the railroad president would equally show that they cared nothing for the citizen, individually or collectively, because aware that they and not he were the government. Certainly such an attempt to corner "the dear people" and the earth and the fulness thereof will break down. It is for us to decide whether we will let it go on till it breaks down of itself, dragging down to die, as a savage dies of his vice, the civilization it has gripped with its hundred hands; or whether, while we are still young, still virtuous, we will break it down, self-consciously, as the civilized man, reforming, crushes down the evil. If we cannot find a remedy, all that we love in the word America must die. It will be an awful price to pay if this attempt at government of the people, by the people, for the people must perish from off the face of the earth, to prove to mankind that political brotherhood cannot survive where industrial brotherhood is denied. But the demonstration is worth even that.

Aristotle's lost books of the Republics told the story of two hundred and fifty attempts at free government, and these were but some of the many that had to be melted down in the crucible of fate to teach Hamilton and Jefferson what they knew. Perhaps we must be melted by the same fierce flames to be a light to the feet of those who come after us. For as true as that a house divided against itself cannot stand, and that a nation half slave and half free cannot permanently endure, is it true that a people who are slaves to market-tyrants will surely come to be their slaves in all else, that all liberty begins to be lost when one liberty is lost, that a people half democratic and half plutocratic cannot permanently endure.

The secret of the history we are about to make is not that the world is poorer or worse. It is richer and better. Its new wealth is too great for the old forms. The success and beauties of our old mutualities have made us ready for new mutualities. The wonder of to-day is the modern multiplication of products by the union of forces; the marvel of to-morrow will be the greater product which will follow when that which is co-operatively produced is co-operatively enjoyed. It is the spectacle of its concentration in the private fortunes of our day which reveals this wealth to its real makers—the whole people—and summons them to extend the manners and institutions of civilization to this new tribal relation.

Whether the great change comes with peace or sword, freely through reform or by nature's involuntary forces, is a mere matter of detail, a question of convenience—not of the essence of the thing. The change will come. With reform, it may come to us. If with force, perhaps not to us. But it will come. The world is too full of amateurs who can play the golden rule as an aria with variations. All the runs and trills and transpositions have been done to death. All the "sayings" have been said. The only field for new effects is in epigrams of practice. Titillation of our sympathies has become a dissipation. We shed a daily tear over the misery of the slums as the toper takes his dram, and our liver becomes torpid with the floods of indignation and sentiment we have guzzled without converting them into their co-efficients of action.

"Regenerate the individual" is a half-truth; the reorganization of the society which he makes and which makes him is the other half. Man alone cannot be a Christian. Institutions are applied beliefs. The love of liberty became liberty in America by clothing itself in the complicated group of structures known as the government of the United States. Love is a half-truth, and kissing is a good deal less than half of that. We need not kiss all our fellow-men, but we must do for them all we ask them to do for us—nothing less than the fullest performance of every power. To love our neighbor is to submit to the discipline and arrangement which make his life reach its best, and so do we best love ourselves.

History has taught us nothing if not that men can continue to associate only by the laws of association. The golden rule is the first and last of these, but the first and last of the golden rule is that it can be operated only through laws, habits, forms, and institutions. The Constitution and laws of the United States are, however imperfectly, the translation into the language of politics of doing as you would be done by—the essence of equal rights and government by consent. To ask individuals to-day to lead by their single sacri-

fices the life of the brother in the world of business is as if the
American colonist had been asked to lead by his individual enterprise the life of the citizen of a republic. That was made possible
to him only by union with others. The business world is full of
men who yearn to abandon its methods and live the love they feel;
but to attempt to do so by themselves would be martyrdom, and
that is "caviare to the general." "We admire martyrdom," Mazzini,
the martyr, said, "but we do not recommend it." The change must
be social, and its martyrdoms have already begun.

New freedoms cannot be operated through the old forms of
slavery. The ideals of Washington and Hamilton and Adams could
not breathe under kingly rule. Idle to say they might. Under the
mutual dependence of the inside and outside of things their change
has all through history always been dual. Change of heart is no more
redemption than hunger is dinner. We must have honesty, love,
justice in the heart of the business world, but for these we must
also have the forms which will fit them. These will be very different
from those through which the intercourse of man with man in the
exchange of services now moves to such ungracious ends. Forms of
Asiatic and American government, of early institutions and to-day's,
are not more different. The cardinal virtues cannot be established
and kept at work in trade and on the highways with the old apparatus. In order that the spirit that gave rebates may go to stay,
the rebate itself must go. If the private use of private ownership of
highways is to go, the private ownership must go. There must be
no private use of public power or public property. These are
created by the common sacrifices of all, and can be rightfully used
only for the common good of all—from all, by all, for all. All the
grants and franchises that have been given to private hands for
private profit are void in morals and void in that higher law which
sets the copy for the laggard pens of legislatures and judges. "No
private use of public powers" is but a threshold truth. The universe,
says Emerson, is the property of every creature in it.

No home so low it may not hope that out of its fledglings one
may grow the hooked claw that will make him a millionaire. To
any adventurer of spirit and prowess in the Italy of the Renaissance
might come the possibility of butchering or poisoning his way to a
castle or a throne. Such prizes of power made the peninsula a
menagerie of tyrants, murderers, voluptuaries, and multitudes of
misery. We got republican liberty by agreeing each with the other

never to seek to become kings or lords or dukes. We can get industrial and economic liberty only by a like covenant never to let ourselves or any one else be millionaires.

There can be no public prosperity without public virtue, and no public virtue without private virtue. But private cannot become public except by organization. Our attempts at control, regulation, are but the agitations of the Gracchi, evidencing the wrong, but not rising to the cure. We are waiting for some genius of good who will generalize into one body of doctrine our partial truths of reform, and will help us live the generalization. Never was mankind, across all lines of race, creed, and institutions, more nearly one in discontent and restless consciousness of new powers and a new hope and purpose, never more widely agitated by influences leading in one direction, never more nearly a committee of the whole on the question of the day. Never before were the means for flashing one thought into the minds of the million, and flashing that thought into action, what they are to-day. The good word or good deed of Chicago in the morning may be the inspiration of Calcutta before nightfall. The crusades were but an eddy in comparison with the universal tide waiting for another Peter the Hermit to lead us where the Man who is to rise again lies in the hands of the infidel.

Our problem can be read from its good side or its bad, and must be read from both, as: Business has become a vice, and defeats us and itself; or, Humanity quickens its step to add to its fellowships the new brotherhood of labor. The next emancipation, like all emancipations, must destroy and build. The most constructive thinker in history said, Love one another; but he also drove the money-changers from the temple, and denounced the scribes and Pharisees, and has been busy for nineteen hundred years pulling down tenements unfit for the habitation of the soul. We see something new and something old. Old principles run into mania, a wicked old world bursting into suicidal explosion, as Carlyle said of the French Revolution. New loves, new capabilities, new institutions, created by the expansion of old ideals and new opportunities of human contact. Our love of those to whom we have been "introduced" is but unlocking a door through which all men will pass into our hearts. What makes men lovable is not the accident of our knowing them. It is that they are men. Before 1776 there were thirteen patriotisms in America.

The word of the day is that we are about to civilize industry. Mankind is quivering with its purpose to make men fellow-citizens,

brothers, lovers in industry, as it has done with them in government
and family, which are also industry. We already have on our shelves
the sciences—hygienic, industrial, political, ethical—to free the
world almost at a stroke from war, accidents, disease, poverty, and
their flowing vices and insanities. The men of these sciences are
here at call praying for employment. The people, by the books they
read, show themselves to be praying to have them put at work.
If we who call ourselves civilization would for one average span
devote to life-dealing the moneys, armies, and genius we now give
to death-dealing, and would establish over the weaker peoples a
protectorate of the United States of Europe and America, we would
take a long step towards settling forever the vexed question of the
site of the Garden of Eden.

"Human nature," "monotony," and "individuality" are the lions
which the reformer is always told will stop the way to a better
world. "You cannot change human nature." There are two human
natures—the human nature of Christ and of Judas; and Christ
prevails. There is the human nature which seeks anonymity, secrecy,
the fruits of power without its duties; and there is the human nature
which rises against these and, province by province, is abolishing
them from human affairs. Men have always been willing to die for
their faith. The bad have died as bravely as the good, Charles I.
with as smooth a front as Sir Harry Vane. In this readiness to die
lies folded every loyalty of life.

"You would make the world a dead level of monotony." Good
society does not think it monotonous that all its women should at
the same time dust the streets with long-tailed gowns, or that its
men should meet every night in funereal black and identical cut,
but it shrinks from the monotony of having all share in reforms
which would equalize surfeit and starvation. "Good society" is still
to come, and it will find some better definition of "monotony" than
a fair share for all—a better definition of variety than too much for
ourselves at the cost of too little for all others. Shall we choose the
monotony of sharing with every one under George III. or Alexander
II. the denial of all right to participate in the supreme power, or
shall we choose the monotony of sharing with every fellow-citizen
the right to become President?—the monotony of being forbidden
to enter all the great livelihoods, some syndicate blocking each way
with "This business belongs to us"? Or the monotony of a democracy, where every laborer has equal rights with all other citizens to
decide upon the administration of the common toil for the common

welfare, and an equal right with every other to rise to be a Captain of Industry? Such are the alternatives of "monotony." We have made an historic choice in one; now for the other.

And "individuality." "You are going to destroy individuality." We can become individual only by submitting to be bound to others. We extend our freedom only by finding new laws to obey. Life outside the law is slavery on as many sides as there are disregarded laws. The locomotive off its tracks is not free. The more relations, ties, duties, the more "individual." The isolated man is the mere rudiment of an individual. But he who has become citizen, neighbor, friend, brother, son, husband, father, fellow-member, in one, is just by so many times individualized. Men's expanding powers of co-operation bring them to the conscious ability to unite for new benefits; but this extension of individuality is forbidden in the name of individuality. There are two individualities: that of the dullard, who submits to take his railroad transportation, his light, his coal, his salt, his reaping-machine at such prices and of such quality as arbitrary power forces upon him, and that of the shrewder man who, by an alliance of the individualities of all, supplies himself at his own price.

In nothing has liberty justified itself more thoroughly than in the resolute determination spreading among the American people to add industrial to political independence. It is the hope of the world that good has its effects as well as evil, and that on the whole, and in the long-run, the seed of the good will overgrow the evil. "Heaven has kindly given our blood a moral flow." Liberty breeds liberties, slavery breeds slaveries, but the liberties will be the strongest stock. If the political and religious liberties which the people of this country aspired to set up had in them the real sap and fibre of a better life than the world had yet known, it must certainly follow that they would quicken and strengthen the people for discovery and obedience in still higher realms. And just this has happened. Nowhere else has the new claim to tax without representation been so quickly detected, so intelligently scrutinized, and so bravely fought. Nowhere else has this spreading plague of selfishness and false doctrine found a people whose average and general life was pitched on so high a level that they instantly took the alarm at its claims over their lives and liberties. It has found a people so disciplined by the aspiration and achievement of political and religious rights that they are already possessed of a body of doctrine capable, by an easy extension, of refuting all the pretensions of the new absolutism. At the very beginning of this new democratic life among the nations it was understood that to be safe liberty must be complete on its industrial as well as on its political and religious sides. This is the American principle. "Give a man power over my subsistence," said Alexander Hamilton, "and he has power over the whole of my moral being." To submit to such a power gives only the alternative of death or degradation, and the high spirit of America preferred then, as it prefers now, the rule of right, which gives life.

The mania of business has reached an acuter and extremer development in America than elsewhere, because nowhere else have bounteous nature and free institutions produced birthrights and pottages so well worth "swapping." But the follies and wickedness of business have nowhere been so sharply challenged as in free America. "Betake yourself to America," said Carlyle to a friend beginning a literary career; "there you can utter your freest thoughts in ways impossible here." It is to this stern wakefulness of a free people that the world owes it that more light has been thrown in America than in any other country on the processes of modern money-making. A free press, organ of a free people, has done invaluable service. The legislatures have pushed investigation after investigation into the ways in which large masses of the people have been deprived, for the benefit of single men or groups of men, of rights of subsistence and government. Through the courts the free people have pursued their depredators by civil and criminal process, by public and private prosecutions. Imperfect and corrupt, these agencies of press, courts, legislatures have often been; they have still done a work which has either been left undone altogether in other countries, or has been done with but a fraction of our thoroughness.

It is due to them that there exists in the reports of legislative investigations, State and national, in the proceedings of lawsuits and criminal trials, in the files of the newspapers, a mass of information which cannot be found in any other community in the world. There is in these archives an accumulation of the raw material of tragedy, comedy, romance, ravellings of the vicissitudes of human life, and social and personal fate, which will feed the fires of whole generations of literary men when once they awake to the existence of these precious rolls. In these pigeon-holes are to be found keys of the present and clews to the future. As America has the newest and widest liberty, it is the stage where play the newest and widest forces of evil as well as good. America is at the front of the forward line of evolution. It has taken the lead in developing competition to the extreme form in which it destroys competition, and in superfining the processes of exchange of services into those of the acquisition of the property of others without service.

The hope is that the old economic system we inherited has ripened so much more rapidly than the society and government we have created that the dead matter it deposits can be thrown off by our vigorous youth and health. "It is high time our bad wealth came to an end," says Emerson. It has grown into its monstrous forms so fast that the dullest eye can separate it from the Commonwealth, and the slowest mind comprehend its mischievousness. In making themselves free of arbitrary and corrupt power in government the Americans prepared themselves to be free in all else, and because foremost in political liberty they have the promise of being the first to realize industrial liberty—the trunk of a tree of which political liberty is the seed, and without which political liberty shrinks back into nothingness.

"The art of Italy will blossom over our graves," Mazzini said when, with true insight, he saw that the first artistic, first literary task before the Italians was to make their country free. Art, literature, culture, religion, in America, are already beginning to feel the restrictive pressure which results from the domination of a selfish, self-indulgent, luxurious, and anti-social power. This power, mastering the markets of a civilization which gives its main energies to markets, passes without difficulty to the mastery of all the other activities. When churches, political campaigns, the expounding of the law, maintenance of schools and colleges, and family life itself all depend on money, they must become servile to the money power. Song, picture, sermon, decrees of court, and the union of hearts must pass constantly under stronger control of those who give their lives to trade and encourage everybody else to trade, confident that the issue of it all will be that they will hold as property, in exclusive possession, to be doled out on their own terms, the matter by which alone man can live, either materially or spiritually.

In America, where the supreme political power and much of the government of church and college have been taken out of traditional hands and subjected to the changing determinations of popular will, it has inevitably resulted that the State, church, and school have passed under this mercantile aristocracy to a far greater extent than in other countries where stiffer regimes under other and older influences still stand. Our upper classes—elected, as always, by the equipoise of effort and opinion between them and the lower classes—are, under this commercial system, the men who trade best, who can control their features and their consciences so that they can always get more than they give, who can play with supply and demand so that at the end of the game all their brethren are their tributaries for life. It is the birthright-buying minds that, by the adoption of this idea, we choose for our rulers. The progressive races have altered their ideals of kings with the indescribable advantage of being ruled by Washingtons and Lincolns and Gladstones instead of Caligulas and Pharaohs. We have now to make a similar step forward in another part of life. The previous changes expressed outwardly an inner change of heart. The reformer of to-day is simply he who, with quicker ear, detecting that another change of heart is going on, goes before.

Another great change is working in the inner mind of man, and will surely be followed by incorporation in institutions and morals and manners. The social head and heart are both being persuaded that too many are idle—rich and poor; too many are hurt in body and soul—rich and poor; too many children are "exposed," as in the old Greek and Roman market-places; too many are starving within reach of too much fertile waste; too many passions of envy, greed, and hate are raging among rich and poor. There is too much left undone that ought to be done along the whole scale of life, from the lowest physical to the highest spiritual needs, from better roads to sweeter music and nobler worship. It cannot be long, historically speaking, before all this new sense and sentiment will issue in acts. All will be as zealously protected against the oppression of the cruel in their daily labor as now against oppression from invader or rioter, and will be as warmly cheered in liberty to grow to their fullest capabilities as laborers—i.e., users of matter for the purposes of the spirit—as they are now welcomed to the liberty of the citizen and the worshipper. Infinite is the fountain of our rights. We can have all the rights we will create. All the rights we will give we can have. The American people will save the liberties they have inherited by winning new ones to bequeath.

With this will come fruits of new faculty almost beyond calculation. A new liberty will put an end to pauperism and millionairism and the crimes and death-rate born of both wretchednesses, just as the liberty of politics and religion put an end to martyrs and tyrants. The new liberty is identical in principle and purpose with the other; it is made inevitable by them. Those who love the liberties already won must open the door to the new, unless they wish to see them all take flight together. There can be no single liberty. Liberties go in clusters like the Pleiades.

We must either regulate, or own, or destroy, perishing by the sword we take. The possibility of regulation is a dream. As long as this control of the necessaries of life and this wealth remain private with individuals, it is they who will regulate, not we. The policy of regulation, disguise it as we may, is but moving to a compromise and equilibrium within the evil all complain of. It is to accept the principle of the sovereignty of the self-interest of the individual and apply constitutional checks to it. The unprogressive nations palter in this method with monarchy. But the wits of America are equal to seeing that as with kingship and slavery so with poverty—the weeding must be done at the roots. Sir Henry Sumner Maine says mankind moves from status to contract; from society ruled by inherited customs to one ruled by agreement, varied according to circumstances. Present experience suggests the addition that the movement, like all in nature, is pendulous, and that mankind moves progressively from status to contract, and from this stage of contract to another status. We march and rest and march again.

We are to have, of course, great political changes. We are to apply the co-operative methods of the post-office and the public school to many other common toils, to all toils in which private sovereignty has become through monopoly a despotism over the public, and to all in which the association of the people and the organization of processes have been so far developed that the profit-hunting Captain of Industry may be replaced by the public-serving Captain of Industry. But we are to have much more. We are to have a private life of a new beauty, of which these are to be merely the mechanical exhibitions on the side of politics. We are to move among each other, able, by the methodical and agreed adherence of all, to do what the words of Lamennais[1] mean, instead of being able, as now, in most things, to afford only an indulgence in feeling them. We are to be commoners, travellers to Altruria.[2]

[1] Lamennais: Félicité Robert De Lamennais (1782-1854). A leading French intellectual and prose stylist of the post-revolutionary era. He was as unconventional in his defense of his Catholic faith as in his attempts to defend liberalism and democracy after he left the Church. [T.C.]

[2] Altruria: *A Traveler from Altruria* (1894) by William Dean Howells which contrasted the Utopian land Altruria with America in the 1890's. [T.C.]

We are to become fathers, mothers, for the spirit of the father and mother is not in us while we can say of any child it is not ours, and leave it in the grime. We are to become men, women, for to all about reinforcing us we shall insure full growth and thus insure it to ourselves. We are to become gentlemen, ladies, for we will not accept from another any service we are not willing to return in kind. We are to become honest, giving when we get, and getting with the knowledge and consent of all. We are to become rich, for we shall share in the wealth now latent in idle men and idle land, and in the fertility of work done by those who have ceased to withstand but stand with each other. As we walk our parks we already see that by saying "thine" to every neighbor we say "mine" of palaces, gardens, art, science, far beyond any possible to selfishness, even the selfishness of kings. We shall become patriots, for the heart will know why it thrills to the flag. Those folds wave the salute of a greater love than that of the man who will lay down his life for his friend. There floats the banner of the love of millions, who, though they do not know you and have never seen you, will die for you and are living for you, doing in a thousand services unto you as you would be done by. And the little patriotism, which is the love of the humanity fenced within our frontier will widen into the reciprocal service of all men. Generals were, merchants are, brothers will be, humanity's representative men.

There is to be a people in industry, as in government. The same rising genius of democracy which discovered that mankind did not co-operate in the State to provide a few with palaces and king's-evil, is disclosing that men do not co-operate in trade for any other purpose than to mobilize the labor of all for the benefit of all, and that the only true guidance comes from those who are led, and the only valid titles from those who create. Very wide must be the emancipation of this new self-interest. If we free America we shall still be not free, for the financial, commercial, possessory powers of modern industrial life are organized internationally. If we rose to the full execution of the first, simplest, and most pressing need of our times and put an end to all private use of public powers, we should still be confronted by monopolies existing simply as private property, as in coal-mines, oil lands.

It is not a verbal accident that science is the substance of the word conscience. We must know the right before we can do the right. When it comes to know the facts the human heart can no more endure monopoly than American slavery or Roman empire.

The first step to a remedy is that the people care. If they know, they will care. To help them to know and care; to stimulate new hatred of evil, new love of the good, new sympathy for the victims of power, and, by enlarging its science, to quicken the old into a new conscience, this compilation of fact has been made. Democracy is not a lie. There live in the body of the commonalty the unexhausted virtue and the ever-refreshened strength which can rise equal to any problems of progress. In the hope of tapping some reserve of their powers of self-help this story is told to the people.